Our Parents: Helen (McKelvey) Kelly and Joseph Kelly,
Felton, Santa Cruz County, California, 1944

Our McKelvey Ancestors

County Donegal, Ireland, and North America

Joyce V. Kelly, Ph.D.

May, 2023

Our Generation: Jim Kelly, Kate Kelly, Joyce Kelly, and Julie (Kelly) DiMaggio, 2006

Residents of a Typical Village in County Donegal, circa 1890

Acknowledgements

Thanks to my brother Jim for his McKelvey research findings and to my sister Kate for editorial suggestions. Thanks to Jason Rodriguez, the founder of Generations Linked, and our fifth cousin once removed, for providing dozens of suggestions and materials. Thanks also to Irish-Canadian *scéalaí* (storyteller) and historian, Steven L. Cameron, for sharing information about our McKelvey ancestors in Lotbinière County, Quebec, Canada; and to Mrs. Chaun Owens-Mortier, a volunteer researcher at the Truckee-Donner Historical Society, for sharing information about our McKelveys in Truckee, California. Thanks to Ken Falk for designing the cover and family trees.

Cover photos:
Top: Mountain Farm (top) and Village (bottom), Cuala Press Prints. Jack B. Yeats, 1871-1957, West Ireland.

Source: Provided by the John J. Burns Library, Boston College, for unrestricted use.
Jack was the best-known Irish artist of the 20th century and the brother of poet William Butler Yeats.

Attributions: This Family History includes extensive quotations, data, maps, and records—all are attributed. Images also are attributed, or they were provided by family members, or they are in the public domain. Black and white photos were colorized using a feature on MyHeritage.com.

Cover Design: Ken Falk Marketing and Communications

ISBN: 978-1-957468-29-7

Our McKelvey Ancestors

Appendices

Prince of Donegal, Celtic Irish Fantasy Art, by Jim Fitzpatrick

No hawk nor hound,
no steer nor steed,
O'Neill gets from me.
No homage yield,
no tribute send,
no vassal clan are we.
If he is lord of Clandeboye
and Chieftan of Tyrone,
yet I am Prince of Donegal,
-let each man hold his own.

Source: <u>https://jimfitzpatrick.com</u>. I emailed Fitzpatrick, requesting permission to inlude his copyrighted image in this Family History. On February 26, 2023, he responded,"Yes. Go ahead."

INTRODUCTION

My brother Jim began researching our four grandparents in 2018 to prepare for a genealogical research trip to Ireland and England the following year. Our mother, Helen (McKelvey) Kelly (1906-1981), had not shared stories about her youth or family, including her father, John M. McKelvey (1885-1935). But, with help from Ancestry.com, FamilySearch.com, and Irish genealogist Linda Keohane, Jim identified our 3x great-grandfather, John McKelvey, who was born in County Donegal in 1771. Jim learned that the McKelveys later immigrated to Quebec, Canada, then to Eau Claire, Wisconsin, and Alpena, Michigan.

I continued Jim's research on the McKelvey's 19th-century lives to identify:[1]

(1) Our earliest great-grandparents.

(2) parishes/townlands in Co. Donegal where our earliest great-grandparents lived;

(3) when and why our McKelvey ancestors left Ireland; and

(4) why they settled in Quebec,[2] what their lives there were like, and when and why they emigrated from Quebec to the United States.

The lack of Irish and Canadian records before the mid-19th century is an insurmountable obstacle to answering these questions definitively. Instead, this Family History summarizes findings and evidence to support **tentative** conclusions. Our failure to document our earliest Irish ancestors is not unique. John Grenham, a well-known Irish genealogist, wrote the following about Irish genealogical research:

> What you will uncover about your family history depends on the quality of the surviving records for the area of origin, on the point from which you start, and the most important ingredient of Irish research, luck. For descendants of Catholic tenant farmers, the limit is generally the starting date of the local Catholic parish records, which varies widely. It would be unusual for records of such a family to go back much earlier than the 1780s, and for most people, the early 1800s is the likely limit . . . the collapse of Gaelic culture in the 17th century, and its subsequent impoverishment and oppression in the 18th century, created an unbridgeable gulf.
>
> https://www.johngrenham.com/browse/retrieve_text.php?text_contentid=513

[1] This History begins in 1800 in County Donegal and ends in 1935 when our maternal grandfather, John Michael McKelvey, died in California.

[2] After 1776, and before Canada's 1840 Act of Union, British North America consisted of Lower Canada (now Quebec) and Upper Canada (now Ontario). In this Family History, British North America is referred to as Canada, Lower Canada is referred to as Quebec, and Upper Canada is referred to as Ontario. Also, English spelling is used. For example, St. Sylvester is St. Sylvestre in French.

Origins of our Irish Ancestors

This is the third of four Family Histories of our grandparents. Our mother's parents were John M. McKelvey (1885-1935), whose grandparents were from County Donegal; and Josephine (Theobald) McKelvey (1880-1937), whose English ancestor immigrated to the British Colony of Virginia in 1641. Our father's parents were Michael Kelly (1869-1944), born in Derrycahill (blue star), County Roscommon; and Mary (Joyce) Kelly (1872/73-1918), born in Loughaconeera (red star), County Galway. The Kelly and Joyce Family Histories are complete; the Theobalds' is forthcoming.

Ireland's 32 counties and 4 provinces[3]

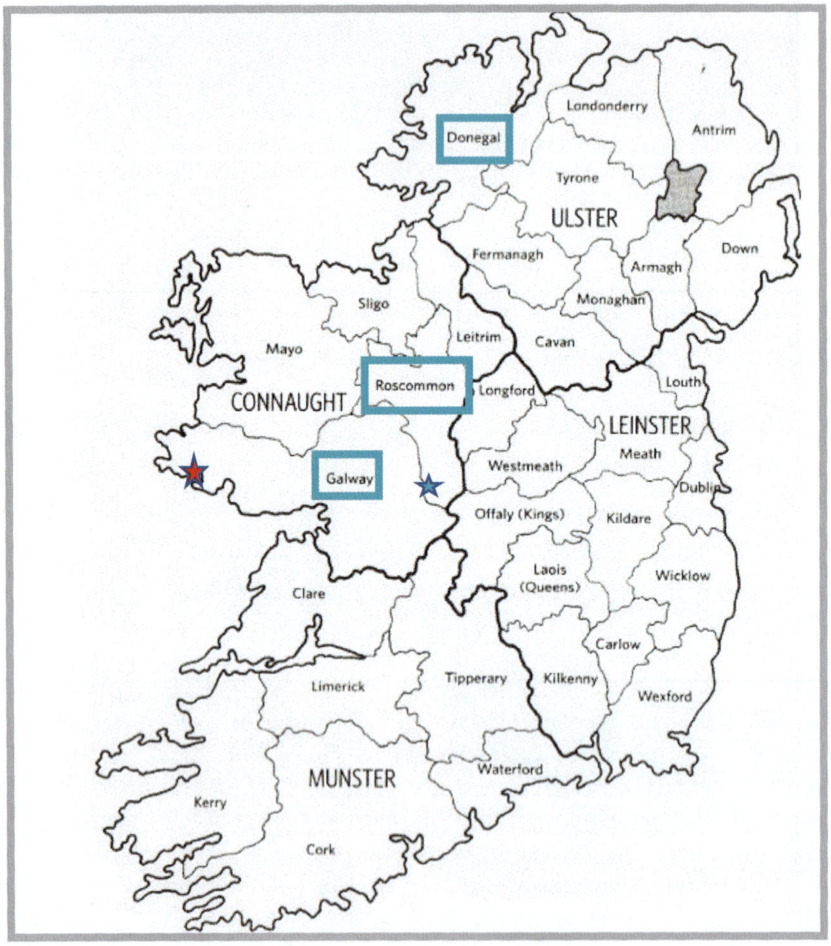

The abbreviated family tree below shows relationships among the McKelveys (this Family History), Kellys, Joyces, and Theobalds, and their Family Histories.

[3] Following partition in 1921, six of nine counties in the northern province of Ulster became "Northern Ireland," a part of Great Britain. The three Ulster counties remaining in Ireland are Donegal, Cavan, and Monaghan.

Abbreviated Kelly/Theobald/McKelvey/Joyce Family Tree

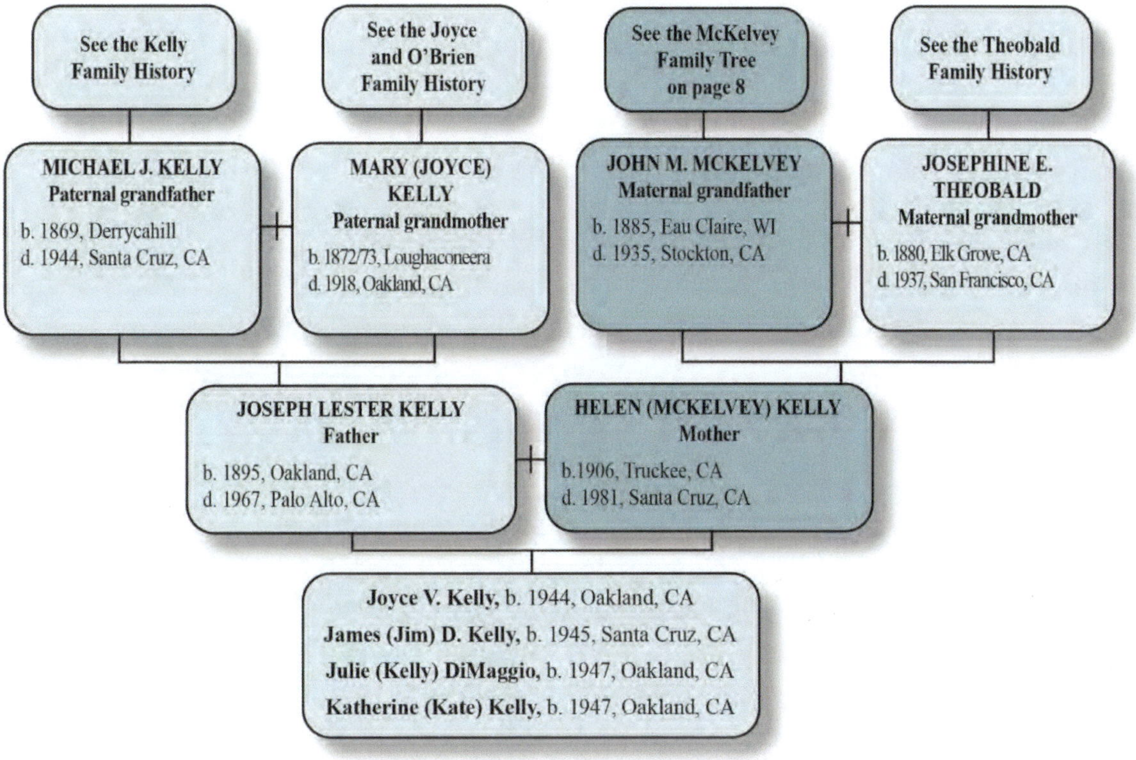

Outline of this Document

This document assembles facts and speculations about our McKelvey ancestors with

(1) a description of early 19th-century County Donegal;

(2) our McKelvey Family Tree, earliest ancestors, and their possible locations;

(3) Irish immigrant life in Quebec, Canada from the 1830s until c. 1875

(4) a list of significant McKelvey family events, with dates and locations;

(5) Ancestry.com profiles of our direct McKelvey ancestors, Appendix One;

(6) evidence for our McKelveys' possible origins within County Donegal, Appendix Two;

(7) Jim's emails from County Donegal while searching for our McKelveys, Appendix Three;

(8) factors that likely motivated our McKelveys to leave Ireland, Appendix Four;

(9) Quebec, Canada: Immigrant life and our McKelveys' villages, Appendix Five;

(10) John and Lawrence McKelvey's Canadian farm and their records, Appendix Six; and

(11) a brief biography of grandfather John M. McKelvey, 1885-1935, Appendix Seven.

EARLY 19TH-CENTURY COUNTY DONEGAL

Located on the northwest coast of Ireland, Donegal faces the Atlantic to the west and north and Lough Foyle to the east. It has peninsulas and inlets with rugged mountains and boglands in the west and fertile valleys in the east. Donegal is called *Dún na nGall* (Fortress of Foreigners) in Irish, reflecting the Viking origin of Donegal Town.

The County was created in 1585 by combining two ancient Gaelic Irish kingdoms. After Britain defeated the Irish in 1602 at Kinsale and the Gaelic Earls fled to Europe in 1607, the Crown seized their land. Britain immediately increased her control over Donegal by granting much of Ulster as "Plantations" to Scottish and British Anglicans. Planters, in turn, were required to recruit settlers from Scotland and England to farm the land and develop garrisons and towns. See Appendix Four.

Like the rest of West Ireland, County Donegal was, and still is, traditional, rural, poor, sparsely populated,[4] and more likely to have Irish-speakers compared to the East. Traditionalism can be partially measured by the prevalence of Irish-language speakers, which, in the past, was inversely related to residents' abilities to read and write. The 1871 map illustrates data collected 35 years after the McKelveys immigrated to Canada.

Prevalence of Irish-speakers in Ireland in 1871 (County Donegal outlined in blue)
Red=>50%; dark pink=25-50%; light pink=0-25%; white=0

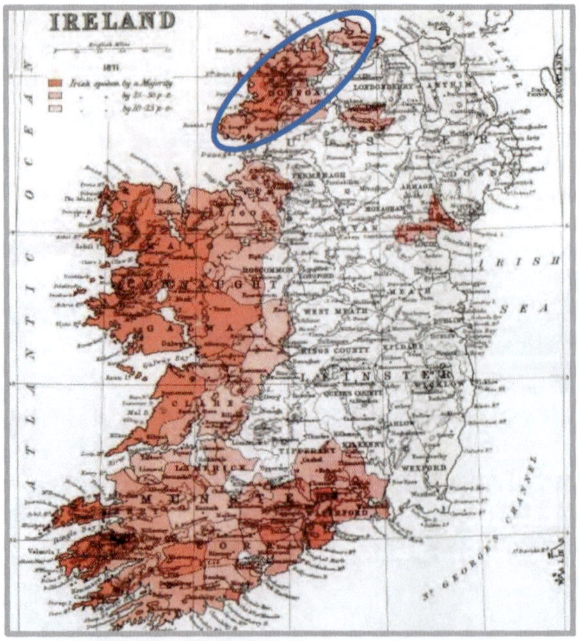

Source: E.G. Ravenstein, "Prevalence of Celtic Languages in 1871," *Journal of the Statistical Society of London*, September 1879, p. 583.

[4] County Donegal is still the third least densely populated county in Ireland. The County's 2022 population was 166,321. Its principal city, Letterkenny, had a 2022 population of 17,586.

The English conducted several country-wide surveys of Ireland[5] in the early 19th century, before our McKelveys emigrated to Canada. The most detailed report on County Donegal is the *Ordnance Survey of 1833-1836.*[6] The Survey was designed to include maps and descriptions ("Memoirs") of every civil (Church of Ireland) parish.

Engineers and soldiers mapped the entire country at six inches to one mile.[7] Prominent local clerics, physicians, and others wrote parish-specific Memoirs. They reported on the local economy and government, landed estates, villages, income, diet, customs and lifestyles of the locals, the practice of religion, and more. But after several years, the Memoir component of the Ordnance Survey was far over budget and abandoned. Memoirs had been completed for every County Donegal parish and five other counties.

To standardize data collection, every memoirist collected information on the same two dozen topics, including those listed below. Excerpts from County Donegal parishes follow.

> Surface and soil: Leaving the moors and mountains in the west and coming to the lowlands, one will see an open, spacious, and fine country, but it would be doing an injustice to the inhabitants of the mountains without remarking on their improvements which are very great, considering the hardship which they endure and labor under. They have drained ditches, broken up and reclaimed barren ground beyond conception, and much as they have done, there is far more to be done if they were able to employ men to assist them.
>
> Crops: The fields produce excellent crops of potatoes, oats, barley, flax and meadow, turnips, and clover, and in many parts, excellent wheat, if the land is rightly prepared.
>
> Housing: They live in low stone cabins with a few small glass windows and thatched roofs bound down with straw ropes. If lime is nearby, cabins may be whitewashed. The cabins consist of 1, 2, or 3 rooms. Those of 2 rooms prevail. They are not clean or comfortable . . . The food of the people is potatoes, water, milk, and some meal. Middle-class farmers also eat butter and eggs, and occasionally, meat or fish. Most people keep a cow and burn turf and a little bog wood. They live from 60 to 80 years and average six in a family.
>
> Labor: The only means that most farmers have of earning money on their farms is by selling their produce, butter, and yarn. This they supply to pay their rent, taxes, and debts, and if they have any to spare, they clothe themselves and their families. The trades in common are blacksmith, carpenter, weaver, tailor, shoemaker, cooper (barrel maker), fuller (cloth dresser), flaxdresser, saddler, slater (maker of slate roofing), and

---

[5] The English surveyed Irish land for future taxation.

[6] *Ordnance Survey, Memoirs of Ireland, Parishes of County Donegal*, vol. 1 and vol. 2 (1833-36), Institute of Irish Studies, Queen's University of Belfast, 1997, reprinted 2021 by the Ulster Historical Foundation.

[7] Brian Fiel's wonderful play, *Translations,* is set in 1833 in the Irish-speaking, fictional village of Baile Beag/Ballybeg in County Donegal during the Ordnance Survey. The play portrays local Irish speakers helping the English surveyors by translating into English, the Irish names of towns and geographic features, e.g. fields and rivers. Source: Brian Fiel, *Translations*, Faber and Faber, London, 1981.

stone mason. The country people convey most of their goods and produce to the market on the backs of donkeys or horses . . . Many go to England and Scotland for harvest and some to the Scotch spinning and carding factories. Only a part of the household leaves home and the others plant the family potatoes for the winter's support.

Education: Children are sent to school at about age 5 years. As they are not constantly kept there, it is a long time before they can read and often lose what they have obtained, on account of the parents being poor and obliged to hire them. There is a general wish for education in all the classes, and parents who are illiterate themselves embrace every opportunity of reaping its advantages . . . but in general they are not able to pay masters.

Convoy Town: Convoy, situated on the principal road from Raphoe to Stranorlar,[8] is the largest village in the Parish of Convoy. Here is placed the parochial church, a Roman Catholic chapel, and a Presbyterian meeting house. There are five public houses, three grocer's shops, a post office, two blacksmith forges, and two bakeries, but no market.

Friendly societies: I regret to state that there are no friendly societies of any kind established in this particular parish for bettering the situation of the poor . . . The farmers are not able (to help the poor) and there are no resident gentlemen.

Emigration: They are beginning to emigrate to America. Most emigrants travel in kinship groups, and in some districts, only industrious members of the community emigrate.[9]

Obstacles to improvement: The chief obstacle to improvements appears to be the absence of landed proprietors on estates, which are too generally exclusively under the management of agents or rather receivers, who have no sympathies with the people, and seem to have one objective, viz. the levy of rent whatever that may be. They make little or no enquiry into the circumstances of the tenantry over whom they are placed.

The total absence of gentry in most parishes means that roads, canals and other means of communication are not improved, and the distance to markets is too great (for tenants to sell their produce). The streams of wealth flowing from the estate to the non-resident landlord are spent in England, and not invested in the estate and its tenants . . . a gentleman residing on his own estate has it greatly in his power to forward, by his own practice, the general improvement of all around.

It cannot be expected that the poor farmer will readily adopt (new farming practices) without the powerful influence of example. His finances are too contracted to hazard experiments. He knows that should such experiments fail; he will face ruin,

Few of them (landlords) are seen amongst us. They hold out no encouragement to their tenants to improve and most of their tenants have neither the means nor the taste to attempt it otherwise . . . [Excerpts from the Ordnance Survey of 1833-1836 for Civil (Church of Ireland) Parishes in County Donegal.]

---

[8] This is one of several areas from which our McKelveys may have originated. **See Appendix Two.**

[9] Ten years later, during the Great Hunger (1845-1852), young, desperate, unskilled, Irish women and men emigrated alone.

Surveyors listed many opportunities for improvement, including urging landowners to improve the quality of life of their tenants by, for example,

(1) building schools and paying schoolteachers' fees;[10]

(2) reducing rents and becoming involved in the lives of their tenants to encourage them, provide examples of improved husbandry, and reduce emigration;

(3) providing tools such as a plough or spade to stimulate industrious tenant farmers;

(4) developing and distributing to tenant farmers, a periodical with Northwest Farming Society news, and extracts from agricultural magazines and newspapers;

(5) transferring ownership of trees to tenants to foster planting and harvesting.

County Donegal farm house, c. 1900

Source: *The Color of Ireland*, Rob Cross, Black and White Publishing, 2021.

MCKELVEY FAMILY TREE

An abbreviated McKelvey family tree is displayed on the next page. For simplicity, this History employs the following surname spellings because they are the most common in our ancestors' records: McKelvey, Slevin, McGuire, and Hagarty.[11] Ancestor.com profiles ("facts") for our direct ancestors are displayed in **Appendix One.**

---

[10] Poor tenant farmers sought education for their children but could not afford to build schools and pay teachers. Only young members of the Anglican Church of Ireland were eligible for free education.

[11] I researched all common surname spelling variants (see **Appendix Two**). Surname spellings varied, even within the same record for the same individual, because most early 19th-century Irish farmers and their families were illiterate and depended on priests, census takers, and others to record their names.

Our McKelvey Ancestors from 1771-1981

JOHN MCKELVEY
Our 3x great-grandfather
b. 1 January 1771, Donegal, County Donegal, Ireland
m. 1806, Ireland
d. 17 May 1860,St. Sylvester, Quebec, Canada

MARY ELLEN SLEVIN
Our 3x great-grandmother
b. 1781, County Donegal, Ireland
m. 1806, Ireland
d. 27 February 1846, St. Sylvester, Quebec, Canada

Lawrence was the third of five children
Catherine m. John Hagarty in Ireland.
In St. Sylvestre, Canada,
Mary m. James Plunkett
Susan m. Francis Gormley
Edward m. Ellen Sheil
Birth/death dates are on the profiles of their parents in Appendix One

LAWRENCE J. MCKELVEY
Our 2x great-grandfather
b. 1812, County Donegal
m. 5 April 1842, St. Sylvester, Canada
d. 17 August 1895, Eau Claire, WI

HANNA MCGUIRE
Our 2x great-grandmother
b. April 1819, County Donegal
m. 5 April 1842, St. Sylvester, Canada
d. 2 October 1909, Lead, SD

John F. was the eldest of 7 children
The names and birth/death dates of their children are on the profiles of their parents in Appendix One

JOHN F. MCKELVEY
Our great-grandfather
b. 23 October 1843, St. Sylvester
m. 6 September 1870, St. Sylvester
d. 18 July 1903, Alpena, Michigan

CATHERINE MONAGHAN
Our great-grandmother
b. 25 February 1849, St. Sylvester
m. 6 September 1870, St. Sylvester
d. 30 August 1928, Alpena, Michigan

John M. was the 5th of 8 children
The names and birth/death dates of their children are on the profiles of their parents in Appendix One

JOHN M. MCKELVEY
Our maternal grandfather
b. 12 January 1885, Eau Claire, WI
m. no records
d. 22 March 1935, Stockton, CA

JOSEPHINE THEOBALD*
Our maternal grandmother
b. 7 July 1880, Elk Grove, CA
m. no records
d. 20 November 1937, San Francisco

HELEN (MCKELVEY) KELLY
Our mother
b. 9 August 1906, Truckee, CA
m. 29 August 1943, Santa Cruz, CA
d. 14 August 1981, Santa Cruz, CA

The McKelvey family emigrated from Ireland to Canada between 1832 – 1836. They emigrated from Canada to the U.S. between 1870 – 1885.
* See "Our Theobald Ancestors" by Joyce Kelly for genealogy and family history. Josephine had two children with William Conner – James and Gertrude, our Mother's half brother and half sister – before she met John McKelvey.

Sources: Records on Ancestry.com are the source of parent-child relationships, events, dates, and locations.

Researched and developed during 2019 - 2023 by Joyce Kelly, incorporating research findings and patrilines from Jim Kelly

Pre-19th Century Irish Records

Beginning in the mid-19th century, events such as births and baptisms of the entire population of Ireland were consistently[12] recorded through civil and church registration.[13] These records are critical for genealogical research because they identify parents, children, and their locations, and they date and locate key events in their lives.

Census records are another vital source of genealogical information. Beginning in 1861, Ireland's decennial Census recorded the names, ages, and other characteristics (e.g., ability to write, languages spoken) of residents of each house. However, Irish Census records are not available before 1901, due to bureaucratic mistakes resulting in the destruction of four decennial Census records from 1861 through 1891. And, with few exceptions, Irish records do not exist before the mid-19th century due to the:

(1) lack of universal civil registration for births, deaths, and marriages before 1864;

(2) lack of universal Catholic church records until the 1829 Emancipation of Catholics;[14] and

(3) Civil War explosion and fire in June 1922 that destroyed the Public Record Office in Dublin,[15] the repository for civil and church records since the 1500s.

In the absence of these records, researchers turn to land records, such as the Tithe Applotment of c. 1830 and Griffith's Valuation of c. 1857 discussed below. But land records lack parent/child relationships and birth and death dates. For example, the Tithe Applotment and Griffith's evaluation list the first and last names of "occupiers" (main tenant/head of household, not entire families) on land throughout the country. Therefore, additional information, such as DNA test results or cluster analysis (Appendix Two), is required to attribute to our ancestral line, a John McKelvey who resided in Ballybofey or elsewhere.

---

[12] Records were maintained for aristocrats and wealthy landowners from before the Middle Ages. Records also were collected for some poor farmers in a few Irish jurisdictions back to the 1500s.

[13] Civil records display births, marriages, and deaths. Church records display baptisms, marriages, and burials. Both types of records include the dates and locations of these events and the names and townland locations of participants, e.g., parents of the newborn or witnesses at a marriage.

[14] We know that our 3x great-grandparents were **Catholic** because they were buried in the cemetery of St. Sylvester Catholic Church in St. Sylvester, Lotbinière County, Quebec. On the 1851 East Canada Census, their son Lawrence reported his religion as Roman Catholic and his occupation as farmer.

[15] A Virtual Record Treasury of Ireland is under development to replace these records. In June 2022, it became available to the public. I searched newly-available Irish records for our McKelveys and their spouses. Several McKelveys and Slevins are included, but the records lack information to link any of these individuals to our ancestral line.

OUR EARLIEST DIRECT MCKELVEY ANCESTORS

When Jim could not extend the McKelvey line before 1771, he hired Irish genealogist Linda Keohane, but she also could not extend the line. Later, I continued Jim's research. This section of the Family History summarizes my research on the question: "Who were our earliest McKelvey great-grandparents and where did they live in County Donegal?"

The family tree on page 8 is an abbreviated version of my full Ancestry.com tree (username joycevkelly66) with more than five dozen McKelveys, spouses, and children born in Ireland, Canada, and the United States. To develop this tree, I searched: (1) AskAboutIreland.ie, (2) Ancestry.com, (3) FamilySearch.org, (4) rootsireland.ie, (5) MyHeritage.com; (6) Findmypast.com; and (7) Canadian and U.S. Census records. Well over 100 family trees on these websites include our McKelvey ancestors.[16] I emailed owners of the most complete trees, but no one extended our McKelvey line before 1771.

I also contacted my matches in the Donegal DNA Match Finder Facebook Group, where I match ten members at 12.1 to 34.2 cMs with Most Recent Common Ancestors (MRCAs) at 4.4 to 5.1 generations. Most matches responded, but we could not identify our MRCAs. GedMatch and Ancestry also display my DNA matches with "cousins" sharing surnames with spouses of several of our earliest McKelveys. However, among those responding to my emails, none had trees extending before 1771. Then, like Jim, I turned to Irish genealogists to validate and extend our McKelvey line:

(1) Joan Patton at Donegal Ancestry, the Irish Family History Foundation Center, reported that they have no early undigitized records for McKelveys or Slevins;

(2) staff in the Family History Division of the National Library of Ireland referred me to websites that index early Irish records, but there were no relevant records; and

(3) Ancestor Network staff (www.ancestornetwork.ie) found and interviewed the inheritor of property in Coolmore[17] belonging to Slevins since before 1850. He provided contact information for the Coolmore Slevins now living in England, and suggested asking them to take DNA tests, but I decided not to proceed.

No source provided information about our pre-1771 McKelvey ancestors.

---

[16] Occasionally, a family tree will include private records with new genealogical information. More commonly, tree makers simply copy information, which may be invalid, from other trees.

[17]Coolmore is 7.7 kilometers (5 miles) north of Ballyshannon, where many Slevins lived (Appendix Two).

Locations of Our Direct McKelvey Ancestors within County Donegal

Records list County Donegal as the birthplace of the two earliest identified generations of direct McKelvey ancestors—our 3x great-grandparents, John (1771-1860) and Mary Ellen Slevin (1781-1846), and our 2x great-grandparents, Lawrence (1812-1895) and Hanna McGuire (1819-1909). I searched for their specific parishes and townlands within County Donegal. **Appendix Two** reports research findings supporting the following speculations about their origins:

1. The **McKelveys** likely originated in the **Donegal Town area and/or between Raphoe[18] and Ballybofey.**[19] This fertile agricultural **area is in, and north of, the Finn Valley; and**

2. the **Slevins and the McGuires** likely originated in the **Donegal Town area, the Finn Valley area**, and/or the **area near Ballyshannon Townland**;

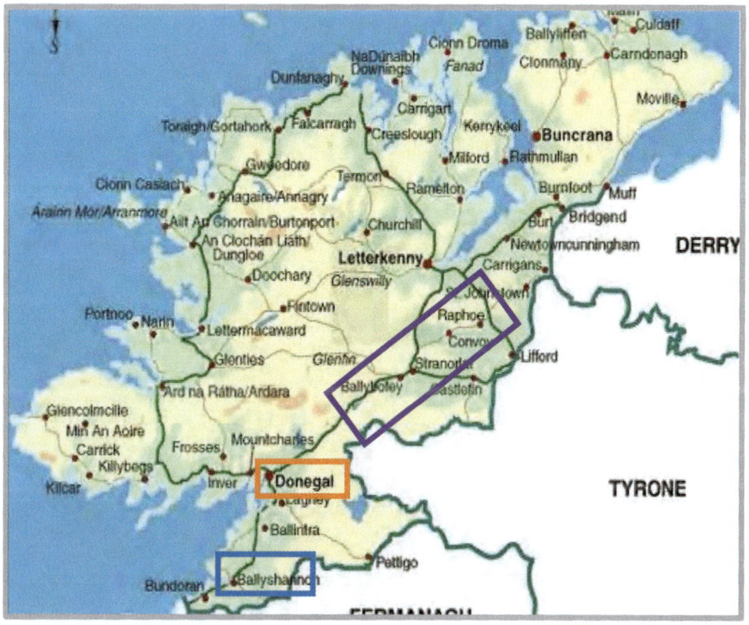

Google map: yellow marks mountains; tan marks peaks; and light green marks farming areas. Most of County Donegal is maritime, remote, mountainous, and poorly suited for farming.

---

[18] Catherine McKelvey (1811-1904), the eldest of John and Mary Ellen's children, married John Hagarty (1804-1890) in Ireland where they had three children. Our fifth cousin once removed, Jason Rodriguez, descends from Catherine and John. Jason's and my Most Recent Common Ancestors are John (1771-1860) and Mary Ellen (Slevin) McKelvey. Undocumented notes from Jason's greatuncle Gaston Haggerty, who travelled to Quebec to research the Haggertys, noted that John Haggerty was from "Raphoe near Letterkenny" suggesting Raphoe Town not Raphoe Parish or Barony. However, none of 211 Griffith's Valuation occupiers with Hegarty/Hagerty/Hagarty/Haggerty surnames lived in Raphoe Parish during Griffith's Valuation (GV) in c. 1857, per GV land records.

[19] **Appendix Three** describes a 2019 family research visit to Ballybofey by Jim and his wife Robin.

The area between Raphoe and Ballybofey includes Convoy and Stranorlar (marked by a red rectangle on the prior page)–all are "Ulster Plantation" (English colonial settlement) towns. Beginning in the early 1600s, King James of Britain sought to Anglicize Ulster, the most Gaelic and independent Irish province. The Crown seized land of native Gaelic chiefs and granted it as "Plantations" to Scottish and English Protestant gentry and soldiers. These settlers were required to build garrisons, and towns around them, to "control" the Irish. Meanwhile, these seizures dispossessed thousands of Irish Catholic landowning farmers. Many chose to remain near their ancestral townlands, often working as tenant farmers for these settlers. **Appendix Two** demonstrates that our earliest direct McKelvey, Slevin, and McGuire ancestors likely lived in the areas of Donegal Town, Ballyshannon, and/or the Finn Valley Area marked with a blue rectangle below. Their land likely was confiscated for "Plantations" in the 17th/18th centuries.

Land Use in County Donegal[20]

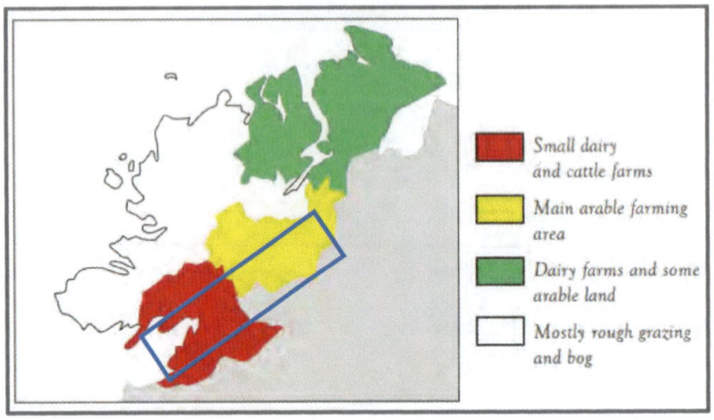

Traditional Unaltered Irish Cottage, c. 1800, County Donegal

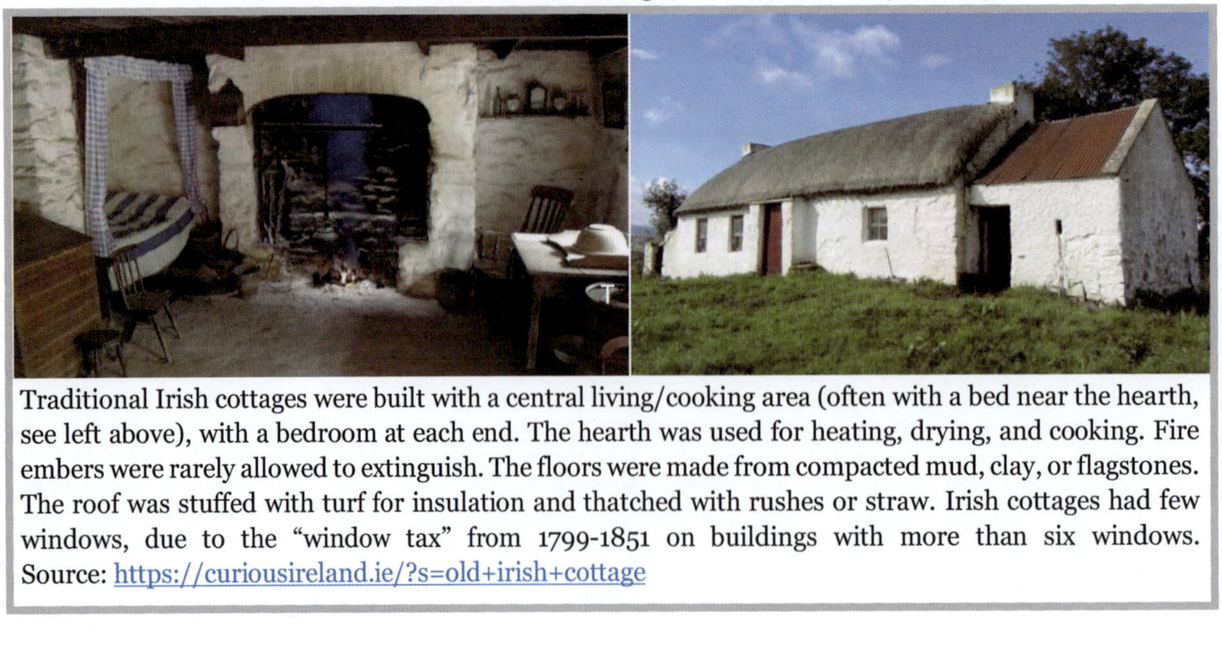

Traditional Irish cottages were built with a central living/cooking area (often with a bed near the hearth, see left above), with a bedroom at each end. The hearth was used for heating, drying, and cooking. Fire embers were rarely allowed to extinguish. The floors were made from compacted mud, clay, or flagstones. The roof was stuffed with turf for insulation and thatched with rushes or straw. Irish cottages had few windows, due to the "window tax" from 1799-1851 on buildings with more than six windows. Source: https://curiousireland.ie/?s=old+irish+cottage

[20] Jonathon Bell and Mervyn Watson developed and displayed this map in their book on farming in Donegal, *Donegal's Farming Heritage*, County Donegal Heritage Office, 2011, 18 pages.

Community Life in 19th-Century Ireland Before the Great Hunger of 1845-1852

Until the 20th-century, Irish tenant farmers kept a turf fire burning continuously for warmth and cooking potatoes. They grew all their food and kept a donkey, chickens, one or more cows for milk, and pigs to raise and sell at local markets. Families spun wool from their sheep, wove cloth, and made their own clothes. Because Catholic churches and schools were illegal from 1659-1829, church services and schools were hidden. Children attended hidden ("hedge") schools until they were old enough to help at home and on the farm. Travelers brought stories and news in exchange for a meal and bedding.

Two Irish historians[21] provided a poignant view of mid-19th century Ireland:

> Over ninety percent of the population lived in clay cabins; survived on a diet of potatoes; and supported a growing population on land that was subdivided with each generation. Farmers' rural settlements (*clachans*) had several dozen one or two room thatch-roofed and mud- or stone-walled cottages, clustered together, housing large families related by blood or marriage.
>
> The families were poor and illiterate, but their villages were self-sufficient with artisans working out of their homes (*clachans* did not have shops, markets, or churches). *Clachans* also had musicians, poets, and storytellers for entertainment. On Sunday afternoons, young people gathered at the crossroads to play and dance. Neighbors met in homes for storytelling. Stories about opportunity and freedom in America were attractive, but the Irish language had no word for voluntary emigration, calling it *deorai* or 'exile.' The most common theme in emigrants' letters was homesickness for families and the rich cultural lives of their villages. (Miller and Wagner, *Out of Ireland-the Story of Irish immigration.*)

Cottages and Hay Stooks, Paul Henry (1877-1958)

19th-century Village in County Donegal

[21] Quoted from *Out of Ireland-the Story of Irish Immigration to America*, by Kerby Miller and Paul Wagner, 1994, Elliott and Clark, Washington DC, pp. 17-19, 25, and 29.

Inniskeen Road: July Evening by Patrick Kavanagh

The bicycles go by in twos and threes
There's a dance in Billy Brennan's barn tonight,
And there's the half-talk code of mysteries
And the wink-and-elbow language of delight.
Half-past eight and there is not a spot
Upon a mile of road, no shadow thrown
That might turn out a man or woman, not
A footfall tapping secrecies of stone.

I have what every poet hates in spite
Of all the solemn talk of contemplation.
Oh, Alexander Selkirk knew the plight.
Of being king and government and nation.
A road, a mile of kingdom. I am king
Of banks and stones and every blooming thing.

Patrick Kavanagh (1904-1967), one of the foremost Irish poets of the 20th century, was born, grew up, and is buried in Inniskeen, a village of 270 people in rural County Monaghan in the Province of Ulster. His father was a shoemaker and farmer. Kavanagh was a poet of ordinary language, writing about everyday life. In this poem, Kavanagh writes about the isolation of the poet during a joyful gathering. Alexander Selkirk (in the poem) was the inspiration for Daniel Defoe's *Robinson Crusoe*. He was a Royal Naval Officer who spent four years as a castaway in the South Pacific.

EMIGRATION FROM IRELAND

Question #3 on page 1 inquires about the McKelveys' emigration dates and reasons to leave their homeland. We cannot verify exact immigration dates because neither Canada nor Ireland collected universal immigration and emigration records[22] until after our McKelveys emigrated. Therefore, I relied on other records (for birth and death dates and locations) and the research of others, including our cousin Jason Rodriguez, to estimate an immigration period of 1832-1836. For example, one Ancestry.com McKelvey family tree[23] displays this undocumented note:

> Sometime between 1832 and 1836, Mary (Slevin) McKelvey (1781-1846), John McKelvey (1771-1860), and their five children emigrated from County Donegal, Ireland to St. Sylvester, Lotbinière County, Quebec, Canada. Their daughter, Catherine, married John Haggerty in Ireland. In St. Sylvester, their daughter Susan married Francis Gromley; daughter Mary married James Plunkett; son Edward married Helen Shields; and son Lawrence married Hanna Maguire. John and Mary were buried in the cemetery of St. Sylvester Catholic Church.
>
> Shortly after Mary Slevin's death, the family moved to Wolfestown, Wolfe County, Quebec. Here Catherine and John Haggerty lived and died. Susan/Francis Gormley, Lawrence/Hanna Maguire, and Edward/Helen Shields settled in Eau Claire, Wisconsin. Susan is buried in the St. Patrick's Cemetery in Eau Claire, Wisconsin, near her daughter-in-law, Roseanna Gromley. Mary and her husband James settled in Alpena, Michigan.

Many of these events, but not their emigration date, are documented on my full "Kelly/Theobald/McKelvey/Joyce family tree on Ancestry.com.[24] Non-subscribers can access this information after establishing a free guest account.

In the absence of personal records, **Appendix Four** of this Family History summarizes 18th- and 19th-century conditions throughout Ireland that prompted millions of farmers, including our extended McKelvey family, to immigrate to North America.

---

[22] Canadian immigration records are incomplete until 1865. Records were maintained at the Gross Ile Quarantine Station, beginning in 1832, and records from some ships show the names of passengers, their departure ports, and their arrival dates and locations. Our ancestors likely arrived at the Port of Quebec City. I searched dozens of immigration lists for Quebec, but none included our McKelvey ancestors.

[23] The current manager of this tree on Ancestry.com told me that the author of this note: (1) no longer responds to questions, and (2) acquired this information from family members many years ago.

[24] See the Ancestry.com profiles ("facts") of our nine direct McKelvey ancestors in **Appendix One,** p. 27. See the KTMJ family tree on Ancestry.com for the profiles with links to their Irish, Canadian, and U.S. records. The tree is under username joycevkelly66 at https://www.ancestry.com/family-tree/tree/160255584?cfpid=282435679566xxxx.

Emigrants sailing from Ireland to North America, 1846

IMMIGRATION TO QUEBEC, CANADA, THEN TO THE UNITED STATES

This section of the Family History addresses the final set of questions on page 1 above: "why did the extended McKelvey family settle in Quebec, Canada, what were their lives like there, and when and why did they emigrate later from Quebec to the United States?"

From the fall of the Gaelic aristocracy in the 17th century until the early 20th century, summer work on farms, canals, and railroads in eastern Ulster, England, and Scotland supported Ireland's economy. To earn money, nearly all adult men in County Donegal worked as summer migrants while old men, women, and children tended the farms at home. This seasonal migration readied the Irish to emigrate permanently.

Emigration to Canada began in the 17th century and increased during the 18th century. After the Napoleonic Wars in Europe ended in 1805, the Canadian government restricted immigration from the United States and encouraged immigration from England and Ireland. Around 1830, 30,000 emigrants arrived annually in Quebec City, the main port of entry to Canada. Approximately two-thirds of these newcomers were from Ireland. By the 1850s, over 500,000 Irish had immigrated to Canada, although many, like our McKelvey ancestors, later joined four million Irish immigrants among 24 million residents in the United States.

Why Immigrate to rural Quebec?

In the absence of records, we must speculate about why the McKelveys immigrated to rural Quebec rather than to the U.S. or England. Six possible reasons come to mind:

First, they could maintain their family-oriented, rural life style by immigrating as an extended family to an area with many Irish Catholic families and affordable land.

Second, authorities encouraged Irish immigration with land grants, low-cost farmland, and other support,[25] without the taxes, and threat of eviction they faced in Ireland.

Third, passenger fares to Canada were much lower than fares to the United States. The British allowed lumber ships returning to Canada to carry more passengers than were allowed on comparably sized American ships, resulting in lower per-person fares.

Fourth, it was relatively easy for immigrants to move from Canada to the United States if the U.S. offered better opportunities in the future.

Fifth, our McKelvey ancestors were practicing Catholics and may have been attracted to Quebec because it was a Catholic province in Protestant North America; and

Sixth, relatives and friends of the McKelveys may have immigrated to Quebec earlier and helped the McKelveys, although I could not find supporting evidence.

McKelveys in Lotbinière County, Quebec, Canada, 1832/1836 to1870/1885

Between 1832 and 1836, our 3x great grandparents John and Mary Ellen McKelvey, and their four unmarried children left County Donegal.[26] In Quebec, each of these children married an Irish immigrant. Two of their four spouses also were from County Donegal, where they may have been acquainted. They emigrated to the Regional County Municipality (RCM) of Lotbinière.[27] Later, most of the McKelveys immigrated to the U.S. between 1870 and 1885. Until then, several dozen McKelvey families, spanning three generations, farmed and logged in Lotbinière and Wolfe Counties of Quebec.

---

[25] See *Advice to Quebec Immigrants* in **Appendix Five.**

[26] John and Mary Ellen's eldest child Catherine, her husband John Hagarty, and their first 3 children immigrated to Quebec in 1836, per Catherine's Canadian Census Records. The Hagartys lived in Wolfestown in Wolfe County, 60 kms (37 miles) SW of St. Sylvester. About 40 years later, when most of the McKelveys immigrated to the U.S., Catherine, John, and 8 of their 10 children stayed in Quebec.

[27] Lotbinière County is in the Chaudière-Appalaches Administrative Area of Quebec. It was, and still is, very rural, with no village of more than 4,000 residents. In 2020, the County's population was 29, 700.

In Lotbinière County, the McKelveys settled near three small villages.

Direct McKelvey Ancestors	Range[28] and Village[29] in Lotbinière County
3x great-grandparents, John (1771-1860) and Mary Ellen (Slevin) (1781-1846)	**St. John's Range, St. Sylvester** (from immigration in 1832/36 to their deaths)
2x great grandparents, Lawrence J. (1812-1895) and Hanna McGuire (1819-1909) They died in Eau Claire, Wisconsin.	St. John's Range, St. Sylvester (from immigration in 1832/36 to immigration to Wisconsin c. 1880.) Hanna lived on her parents' farm in **St. Gilles** until she married Lawrence in 1842 in St. Sylvester. On the 1881 Canadian census, Lawrence and Hanna lived on St. John's Range, **St. Patrice de Beaurivage** (see footnote #29 below).
Great-grandparents, John F. (1843-1903) and Catherine Monaghan (1849-1928). They died in Alpena, Michigan	John was born on St. John's Range, St. Sylvester. Catherine lived on her parents' farm in St. Sylvester until she married John in 1870 and moved to the McKelveys' farm on St. John's Range.

Farm Scene, Eastern Townships of Quebec, south of Lotbinière, by Henry Bartlett, 1840

[28] A range (*rang* in French) is a rectangular piece of land off a perpendicular road (see map on p. 20).

[29] Steve Cameron (p. 20) shared 19th-century-Canadian land and Census records showing that Lawrence McKelvey lived on St. John's Range (next page) in Lotbinière County from before the 1850s until at least 1881.According to Steve, this Range was in the *Seigneurie* (footnote 30) of St. Gilles until 1818, when the township and Catholic Church of St. Sylvester were established. Thus, Lawrence initially lived in St. Sylvester. In 1871, St. Patrice Township and Catholic Church were established in the part of St. Sylvester where Lawrence lived. Therefore, on the 1881 Census, Lawrence lived in St. Patrice. Cameron's records show the McKelveys continuously living on the same farm on St. John's Range.

Lotbinière Co. is outlined in red. Municipalities near McKelveys are circled.

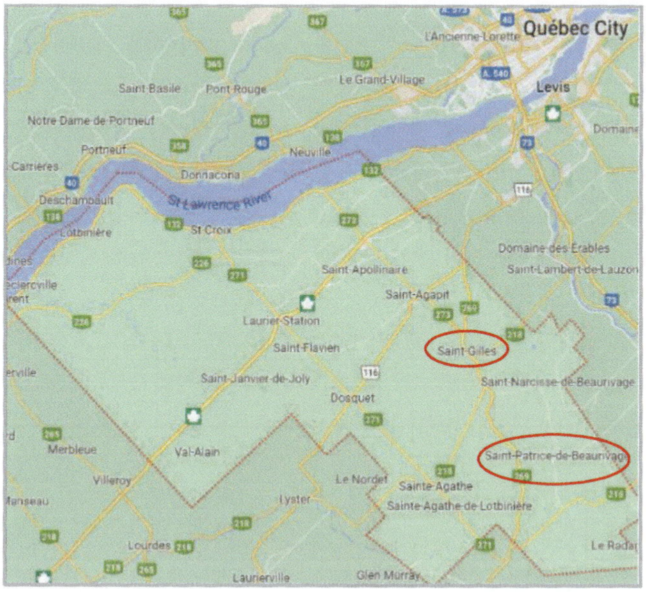

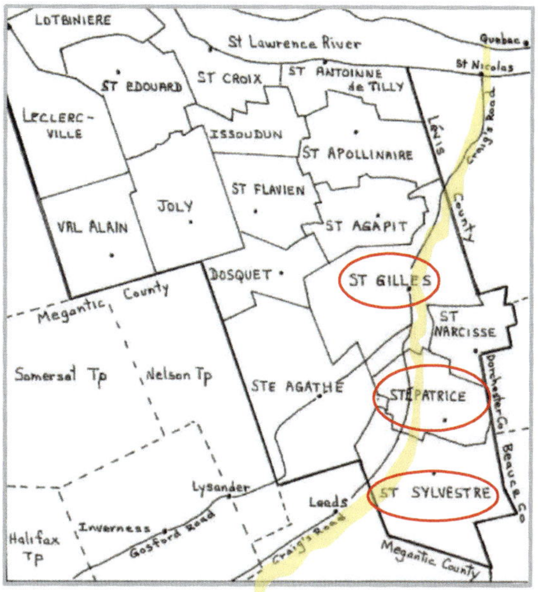

Sources: Left: Google maps. Right and below: Gwen Barry's website at http://www.booksbygwen.ca

The families of John and his son, Lawrence McKelvey, lived on a farm in St. John's Range (red rectangle below and map on the next page) during their entire stay in Quebec, from c. 1832 to c. 1885. Red ovals mark the villages of St. Sylvester and St. Patrice near St. John's Range. Families of John's other children lived in St. Gilles and in Wolfestown in Wolfe County (not on the maps). The yellow line marks Craig's Road, discussed below. The distance between St. Gilles and St. Sylvester is 23 kms or 14 miles. Early Irish settlers, who arrived at least 20 years before the McKelveys, established their farms near Craig's Road which had the best farmland and access to markets.

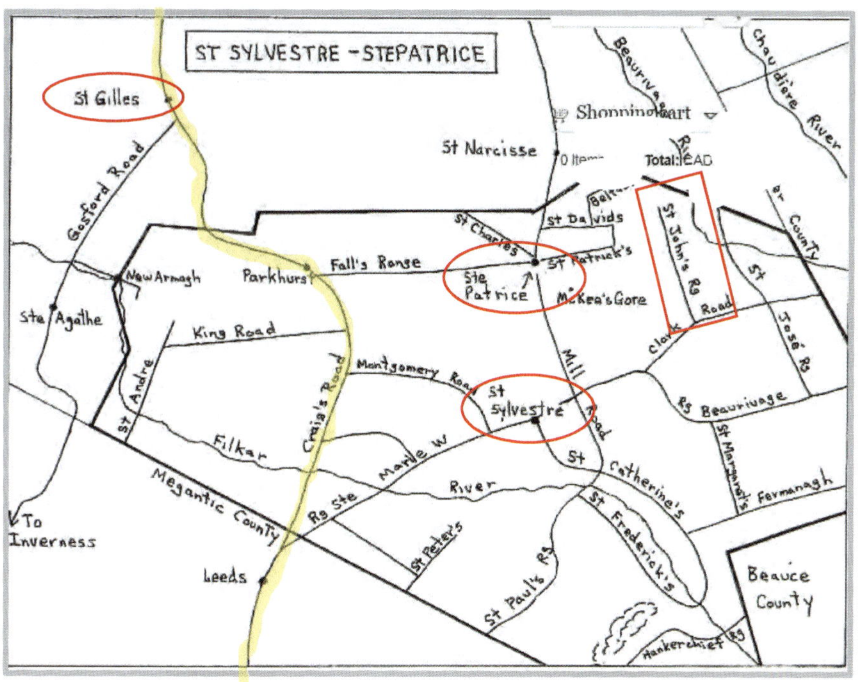

Lots on St. John's Range (red rectangle above), c. 1870.

Farms in the ranges typically were long narrow strips with public roads on both ends (see dark lines on the left and right on the map below). Lawrence McKelvey's farm is marked in orange. The Gormley farms are in blue. (Lawrence's sister Susanna married Francis Gormley Sr. James and Thomas may be Francis's brothers, but this could not be confirmed). The farms of Lawrence's brothers-in-law, John and Michael Hearn, are in green. (Their sister, Mary Anne Hearn, married James McGuire, the brother of Lawrence's wife Hanna McGuire). Also, Mary Anne and James's daughter, Mary Anne, married Francis Gormley Jr. See my Ancestry family tree for documentation. These intermarriages are consistent with Steve Cameron's obervation that many Irish-Canadian marriages occurred among families living within a 30 minute walk.

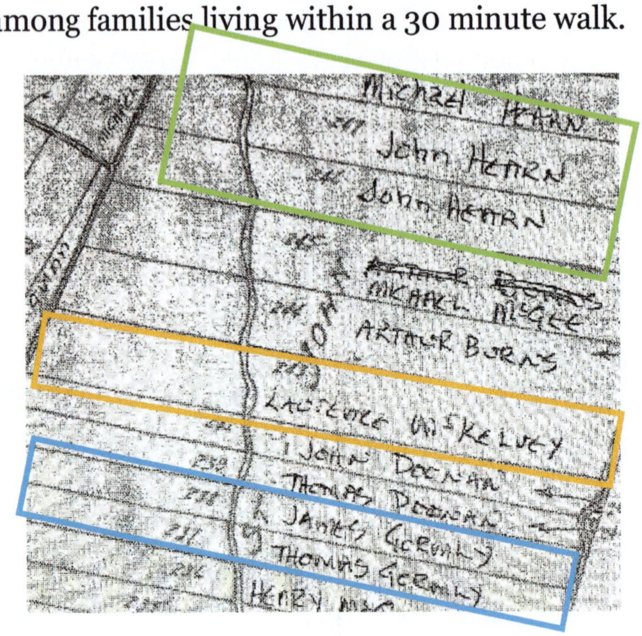

Source and comments: Steve Cameron created this map by copying onto a 19th-century land map, the names of landowners, obtained directly from Surveyor O'Sullivan's c. 1870 original register. Above the top of this map is a lot (not shown) belonging to Matthew Plunkett, b. 1848. Matthew is the son of James Plunket, b. 1812 (another of Lawrence's brothers-in-law), Steve located a record showing that James purchased land on St. John's Range in 1840. Thus, by 1870, Matthew had acquired the land purchased by his father in 1840.

Early History of St. Sylvester in Lotbinière County, Quebec

Scéalaí (storyteller), historian, and genealogist, Steven L. Cameron, was born in Montreal and lives near St. Sylvester. He is a fifth-generation Irish-Canadian and published three books about 19th-century Irish settlers in St. Sylvester. These books describe daily life and extraordinary events (e.g., 5 murders!) between 1832/36 and 1870/85, when our McKelvey ancestors lived there. These passages are from his books:

The Native American Abenaki had been seasonal visitors . . . They had been pushed north and west from their original New England home and settled between the Canadian/U.S. border and the St. Lawrence River, constantly moving for food.

The first settlement of St. Sylvester was along **Craig's Road** (a main thoroughfare and bloodline during the 19th century) . . . By 1824, there were 214 families of Irish, French Canadian, English, and Scotch settlers in the area. This mixed demographic changed significantly with the arrival of a large wave of Catholic and Protestant Irish settlers during the mid-1820s to mid-1830s.Settlement commenced north-to-south and east-to-west. The topography of St. Sylvester was 'rough.' The northeastern area was approximately 500 feet above sea-level, but the south and south-western areas climbed to hills 2200-2500 feet above sea level. Roads were really little more than horse-paths.

The settlement of difficult terrain was further rushed by a significant outbreak of cholera in Quebec City in 1831/1832 . . . the government immigration agent had immigrants by-pass cholera-infected Quebec City . . . One of the destinations he suggested was the virgin territory along Craig's Road . . . almost all of the incoming settlers to St. Sylvester were of Irish origin. **By 1855**, the ranges were full, land was at a premium . . . and **the population of St. Sylvester was approximately 3,725.** Over 75% of these were Catholic (2/3 Irish, 1/3 French).

A Catholic church was established in St. Sylvester village by 1828. From 1836-1851, it was led by the influential Father James Nelligan from Dingle in County Derry (*photo on page 23 of this Family History*). Father Nelligan was fluent in English, French, Latin, Greek, and Irish . . . Other denominations were served by Churches on **Craig's Road**.

Sources: Steven L. Cameron's wonderful books about the area around St. Sylvester are: *Hill Search, The Robert Corrigan Story*, 2014; *Hill Tales, Still Searching*, 2015, and *Hill Notes, Glimpses of Before*, 2017. I excerpted text from all three books, especially *Searching*, pp. 13-14. Cameron's books are available on Amazon.com.

Irish Pioneers in Quebec

Lucille H. Campey has written fourteen books about Canadian immigrants, including *Ontario and Quebec's Irish Pioneers–Farmers, Labourers, and Lumberjacks,* Dundren Press, Toronto, 2018. To make land accessible to immigrants, she credits 1820s legislation offering freehold tenure (sale)[30] and the building of Craig's Road. Campey wrote about 19th-century Irish Catholic immigrants in Quebec:

[30] In the 1700s, when France controlled Canada, land along the St. Lawrence River was granted to French-Canadian gentry as feudal lands or *seigneuries*. (Before Craig's Road, the River was the only route for transport and communication). The *seigneurial* system was established in 1627 and lasted until the 1800s when the government modernized land distribution. First, *seigneurs* were allowed to sell their land to immigrant farmers via long-term leases that eventually transferred ownership. And second, the government acquired undeveloped land and granted or sold it (through freehold tenure at a low cost) to immigrant farmers. This land became accessible through the newly built Craig's Road.

Irish settlers occupied vacant land on south of Quebec City behind long-settled French communities along the river. With new roads, these areas became accessible . . . jobs in the timber trade and shipbuilding were plentiful . . . Knowledge of the regions's economic potential spread in Ireland and Quebec . . . Alexander Buchanan, the Quebec Immigration Agent . . . noted that Lotbinière County encouraged new settlers . . .

Following the large increases in tariffs on European timber duirng the Napolionic Wars, Canadian timber had a considerable cost advantage, and trade with Ireland soared. Now, as news filtered back to Ireland of good farming opportunities in mid-Canada, the Irish sailed (in returning timber ships) to the fledging communities established by their family and friends. Funds for ship crossings were raised by immigrants and family already settled in Canada. This cooperative spirit produced communities with a shared culture and values.(Lucille H. Campey, *Ontario and Quebec's Irish pioneers*, 2018).

Life on Irish-Canadian Subsistence Farms in Lotbinière, Canada during the 1800s[31]

Farming in 19th-century rural Quebec was not profitable for most Irish immigrants.[32] The growing season was short; winter brought up to 20 feet of snow; and much of the land was hilly and not fertile. Further, subsistence farmers could not obtain credit to pay their bills, diversify their crops, and improve their livestock. To cover expenses, men worked in distant logging camps when they were not farming. Women stayed home to take care of the children, livestock, house, and garden. They preserved food, cooked, cleaned, made clothes, and laundered. Our early ancestors were not literate, so children were not educated until small local schools were established in every range.

Bush Farm in Upper Canada (Ontario), Philip Brainbridge (1817-1881), from Wikicommons

[31] Thank you to Steve Cameron for writing wonderful books, and for sharing information and photos. See next page and Coirneal Cealteach's Facebook page.

[32] Earlier Irish Protestant settlers claimed the most fertile, flat land, close to Craig's Road. Our late-arriving McKelveys settled on St. John's Range, far from the Road, at 2,400 feet above sea level.

Celtic Memorial Cross built by Coirneal Cealteach[33] **Covered bridge across a range river**

See **Appendix Five** for descriptions in French of the histories of St. Sylvester, St. Gilles, and St. Patrice, developed by the Agente de developpement culturel de la MRC de Lotbiniere. Appendix Five also contains excerpts from the following essays about mid-19th-century rural Quebec.

(1) *Advice to Irish Settlers in Quebec, 1832*, by A.G. Buchanan, Chief of Immigration Services. *Advice* was distributed in Ireland and Quebec. It provided useful information, such as the government will supply materials for your first log cabin. *Advice* also listed how and where to obtain help with traveling to where land is available, and more;

(2) the role of the Catholic Church in 19th-century rural Quebec. This essay describes occasional tensions in the generally friendly relations between Irish Catholic immigrants and members of the French-dominated Catholic Church in Quebec; and

(3) the development of an Irish Catholic identify in Beaurivage, an area that includes St. Sylvester. When our McKelveys lived there, Irish Catholics far outnumbered French

[33] **Upper left**: Coirneal Cealteach, co-founded by Steve Cameron, is a non-profit society supporting the heritage of Lotbinière's Irish immigrants. **Lower left**: Father James Nelligan, 1804-1866, see page 21. **Center:** Migrant seasonal workers (many from Quebec) in a New Hampshire lumber camp, 1910-1920. **Right:** Jack Scallion (1869-1953), an Irish-speaking fiddler, and the last itinerant musician in Lotbinière.

Catholics and relationships between the two groups were friendly. But, as the French population grew, few Irish Catholics assimilated. This likely influenced most of our direct ad indirect McKelvey ancestors to immigrate to the U.S., discussed below.

See **Appendix Six** for photos of the McKelvey farm and copies of Canadian records, provided by Steve Cameron: (1) John McKelvey's (1771-1860) Will; (2) property records of Lawrence McKelvey (1812-1895); and (3) Lawrence's U.S. Immigration record.

Departure from rural Quebec

Beginning c. 1855, in addition to poverty, debt, and infertile land, overpopulation pushed Irish-Canadians to leave Quebec. Farmland was no longer available for children of Irish pioneers.[34] It also became clear that French Canadians would dominate Lotbinière County, creating an Irish minority.[35] Finally, after 1850, the upper Midwest was accessible by train, and earlier Irish-Candian immigrants welcomed newcomers.

By the mid-1870s, thousands of Irish-Canadian farmers had left Quebec for New England and the midwestern U.S. where they found Irish immigrant family and friends, as well as fertile farmland, high-paid jobs in nearby logging camps, electricity, and running water–benefits not available in rural Quebec. Between c. 1870 and 1885,[36] four of John and Mary Ellen's five children and their spouses [all but Catherine (McKelvey) Hagarty and her husband John] immigrated to farming communities already established by Irish-Canadians in Eau Claire, Wisconsin. Further, more than 20% of John and Mary Ellen's 49 grandchildren also immigrated to or near Eau Claire. Nearly 50% of the grandchildren immigrated elsewhere in the U.S., and 30% (including 8 of the Hagarty grandchildren) remained in Quebec.

DIRECT MCKELVEY ANCESTORS' TIMELINE, 1771-1981

The table on the next page, developed from my McKelvey Family Tree on Ancestry.com, displays signficant events, dates, and locations of our direct McKelveys from 1771-1981.

[34] The population of Quebec increased by 80% from 335,000 in 1815 to 600,000 in 1840.

[35] According to Steve Cameron, *Hill Search*, p. 13, in 1855, the population of St. Sylvester was 3,725 people. In 2016, the population was 978 and 98% spoke only French.

[36] Civil registration, land, Canadian and U.S. Census records and other family trees on Ancestry.com indicate that McKelveys immigrated, initially to Eau Claire, Wisconsin, at different times between 1870 and 1885. For example, an 1870 U.S. Federal Census record shows that a McGuire nephew of our 2x great-grandmother Hanna (McGuire) McKelvey, hosted McKelvey cousins in Eau Claire. And our 2x great-grandfather, Lawrence, entered the U.S. at Port Huron, Michigan in 1881. He likely traveled on the Grand Truck Railroad from Quebec to Toronto, and from there to Port Huron. See **Appendix Six.**

Direct McKelvey Ancestors' Timeline

Date	Location	Event
1771	**County Donegal, Ireland**	Birth of 3x great-grandfather John
1781	Same	Birth of 3x great-grandmother Mary Ellen Slevin
1812	Same	Birth of 2x great-grandfather Lawrence
1819	Same	Birth of 2x great-grandmother Hanna McGuire
1832-1836*	Immigration to Canada included more than a dozen direct and indirect McKelvey ancestors.	Immigration dates are based on birth and marriage dates and locations, and Canadian Census and land records.
1842	**St. Sylvestre, Lothiniere County, Quebec**	Marriage of 2x great-grandparents Lawrence and Hanna McGuire
1843	Same	Birth of great-grandfather John F.
1846	Same	Death of 3x great-grandmother Mary Ellen Slevin
1849	Same	Birth of great-grandmother Catherine Monaghan
1860	Same	Death of 3x great-grandfather John
1870	Same	Marriage of great-grandparents John F. and Catherine Monaghan
1870-1885	**Eau Claire, Eau Claire County, Wisconsin**	Immigration dates are based on birth, marriage, death, U.S. Census, and Canadian land records. John F.and Catherine likely immigrated in 1870 John's father Lawrence immigrated in 1881.
1885	Same	Birth of grandfather, John Michael.
1895	Same	Death of 2x great-grandfather Lawrence
1903	**Alpena, Alpena County, Michigan**	Many McKelvey ancestors moved from Wisconsin to Michigan between 1885 and 1900 Death of great-grandfather John F.
1906	**Truckee, Nevada County, California**	Birth of our mother Helen J.
1909	**Eau Claire, Eau Claire County, Wisconsin***	Death of 2x great-grandmother Hanna McGuire.
1928	**Alpena, Alpena County, Michigan**	Death of great-grandmother Catherine Monaghan
1935	**Stockton, California**	Death of grandfather John M.**
1981	**Santa Cruz, California**	Death of our mother Helen J. (McKelvey) Kelly

Appendix One displays data sources on Ancestry.com profies for our nine direct McKelvey ancestors. Data sources for indirect McKelvey ancestors are displayed on my Ancestry.com family tree, under username joycevkelly66.

*Hanna McGuire was living with her daughter in Lead, South Dakota when she died. She was buried in Eau Claire. ** Our maternal grandfather John M. McKelvey was the last male in our diect McKelvey line.

John M. McKelvey (1885-1935), the father of our mother Helen (McKelvey) Kelly (1906-1981), moved from Alpena, MI to Truckee, CA in c. 1900 to work with his older brother, Lawrence. There, he met our grandmother Josephine (Theobald) Conner McKelvey (1880-1937). John was Josephine's second "husband," although we could not locate a marriage certificate.

When married to her first husband, William Conner, Josephine had two children–our uncle James Conner and aunt Gertrude (Conner) Reubold. Our mother did not speak of her father nor did she tell us children that Jimmie and Gertie were not her full brother and sister. Aunt Gertie told me that her father, William Conner, owned a ranch[37] in Sacramento County in Northern California, where John McKelvey worked as a ranch hand. Our grandmother Josephine left William to live with John. They lived in Truckee, Nevada County, CA where our mother was born. Sometime later, Josephine, John, our mother, and her brother James moved to San Francisco, where Josephine ran a boarding house. By 1917, John had returned to Truckee, where he lived with or near his brother Lawrence until he died in 1935. **Appendix Seven** provides John's biography.

Appendices

Appendix One	Ancestry.com profiles of our nine direct McKelvey ancestors.
Appendix Two	Evidence about origins within County Donegal of our McKelvey ancestors. This evidence supports possible identification of their ancestral Irish parishes and townlands, see page 11.
Appendix Three	Jim's 2019 emails from County Donegal while searching for our McKelveys in Ballybofey, a possible ancestral townland.
Appendix Four	Events in Ireland that likely motivated the McKelveys to emigrate. These events traumatized Irish communities and caused one-half of Ireland's population to emigrate or perish between 1800 and 1900.
Appendix Five	Irish immigrant life in Quebec and in our McKelveys' villages.
Appendix Six	John and Lawrence's Canadian farm, and land, will, and U.S. immigration records.
Appendix Seven	A brief biography of our grandfather, John M. McKelvey, 1885-1935.

[37] Our brother Jim located records indicating the William Conner did not own the ranch where he worked.

Appendix One

Ancestry.com Profiles of our Direct McKelvey Ancestors, 1771-1981

The Kelly/Theobald/McKelvey/Joyce Family Tree on Ancestry.com (username joycevkelly66) https://www.ancestry.com/family-tree/tree/160255584?cfpid=282435679566 identifies direct and indirect ancestors on our McKelvey line. On Ancestry.com, you can view the tree, individual profiles of facts, and records supporting those facts for our McKelvey ancestors. (I did not fully research every indirect McKelvey ancestor. Therefore, many of their profiles are incomplete).

The abbreviated McKelvey family tree on page 8 above shows relationships among our ancestors. Our nine direct McKelvey ancestors begin with our 3x great-grandparents, John McKelvey (1771-1860) and Mary Ellen (Slevin) McKelvey (1781-1846) and end with our mother, Helen J. (McKelvey) Kelly (1906-1981). Their Ancestry profiles of facts are displayed next.

Profiles of Our Nine Direct McKelvey Ancestors

Relationship	Direct Ancestor	Page Number
Our 3x great-grandparents	John McKelvey (1771-1860)	28
	Mary Ellen (Slevin) McKelvey (1781-1846)	29
Our 2x great-grandparents	Lawrence J. McKelvey (1812-1895)	30
	Hanna (McGuire) McKelvey (1819-1909)	31
Our great-grandparents	John F. McKelvey (1843-1903)	32
	Catherine (Monaghan) McKelvey (1849-1928)	34
Our grandparents	John M. McKelvey (1885-1935)	36
	Josephine (Theobald) McKelvey (1880-1937)	38
Our mother	Helen J. (McKelvey) Kelly (1906-1981)	40

John McKelvey

BIRTH 1 JANUARY 1771 • Donegal, County Donegal, Ireland
DEATH 17 MAY 1860 • Saint-Sylvestre, Lotbeniere County., Quebec, Canada

3rd great-grandfather

Year (AGE)	Fact
1771	**Birth** 1 January 1771 • Donegal, County Donegal, Ireland 1 source
1806 35	**Marriage** Abt. 1806 • Ireland Mary Ellen (Slevin) McKelvey (1781-1846)
1860 89	**Death** 17 May 1860 • Saint-Sylvestre, Lotbeniere County., Quebec, Canada 2 sources
1860	**Burial** 1860 • Saint-Sylvestre Cemetery, Chaudiere-Appalaches Region, Quebec, Canada 2 sources

⊕ Add fact

Ancestry sources

- Ancestry Family Trees
- Canada, Find A Grave Index, 1600s-Current
- Quebec, Canada, Vital and Church Records (Drouin Collection), 1621-1968

Search on Ancestry

⊕ Add source

⊕ Add web link

Parents

- Add father
- Add mother

Spouse and children

- **Mary Ellen (Slevin) McKelvey** 1781–1846
  - **Catherine Mary (McKelvey) Hagarty** 1805–1904
  - **Edward McKelvey** 1810–1892
  - **Lawrence J. McKelvey** 1812–1895
  - **Mary A. (McKelvey) Plunket** 1818–1900
  - **Susanna (McKelvey) Gormley** 1825–1901

Mary Ellen (Slevin) McKelvey

BIRTH 01 JANUARY 1781 • County Donegal, Ireland
DEATH 27 FEBRUARY 1846 • Saint-Sylvestre, Lotbiniere County, Quebec, Canada

3rd great-grandmother

1781 (AGE)	**Birth** 01 January 1781 • County Donegal, Ireland 1 source
1806 25	**Marriage** Abt. 1806 • Ireland John McKelvey (1771–1860)
1846 65	**Death** 27 February 1846 • Saint-Sylvestre, Lotbiniere County, Quebec, Canada 2 sources
1846	**Burial** 1846 • Saint-Sylvestre Cemetery, Lotbiniere County, Quebec, Canada 2 sources

⊕ **Add fact**

Ancestry sources

- Ancestry Family Trees
- Canada, Find A Grave Index, 1600s-Current
- Quebec, Canada, Vital and Church Records (Drouin Collection), 1621-1968

Search on Ancestry

⊕ **Add source**

⊕ **Add web link**

Parents

- **Add father**
- **Add mother**

Spouse and children

- **John McKelvey** 1771–1860
  - **Catherine Mary (McKelvey) Hagarty** 1805–1904
  - **Edward McKelvey** 1810–1892
  - **Lawrence J. McKelvey** 1812–1895
  - **Mary A. (McKelvey) Plunket** 1818–1900
  - **Susanna (McKelvey) Gormley** 1825–1901

Lawrence J. McKelvey

BIRTH 1812 • County Donegal, Ireland
DEATH 17 AUGUST 1895 • Eau Claire, Eau Claire County, Wisconsin
2nd great-grandfather

1812 (AGE)
Birth
1812 • County Donegal, Ireland
3 sources

1842 30
Marriage
5 Avril 1842 • Saint-Sylvestre, Québec, Canada
Hannah McGUIRE (1819–1909)
1 source

1851 39
Residence
1851 • Lotbinière, Canada East (Quebec), Canada
Religion: Roman Catholic
1 source

1881 69
Residence
1881 • St Patrice de Beaurivage, Lotbinière, Quebec, Canada
Marital Status: Married
1 source

1885 73
Residence
1885 • Eau Claire, Eau Claire County, Wisconsin
1 source

1891 79
Residence
1891, 1892 • Eau Claire, Eau Claire County, Wisconsin
1 source

1895 83
Death
17 August 1895 • Eau Claire, Eau Claire County, Wisconsin
1 source

1895
Burial
18 August, 1895 • St. Patrick's Cemetery, Eau Claire, Eau Claire County, Wisconsin

Ancestry sources

- 1851 Census of Canada East
- 1881 Census of Canada
- Eau Claire, Wisconsin Directories, 1889-93
- Quebec, Canada, Vital and Church Records (Drouin Collection), 1621-1968
- U.S. City Directories, 1822-1995
- U.S., Find A Grave Index, 1600s-Current

Search on Ancestry
Add source
Add web link

Parents

- John McKelvey 1771–1860
- Mary Ellen Slevin 1781–1846

Siblings

Spouse and children

- Hannah McGUIRE 1819–1909
  - John F. McKelvey 1843–1903
  - Hanna McKelvey 1845–1861
  - Mary Anne McKelvey 1847–1941
  - Patrick McKelvey 1854–1912
  - Cecelia Agnes McKelvey 1860–1946
- Margaret Jane "Maggie" McKelvey 1865–1903
- Susan McKelvey 1868–1938

Add family

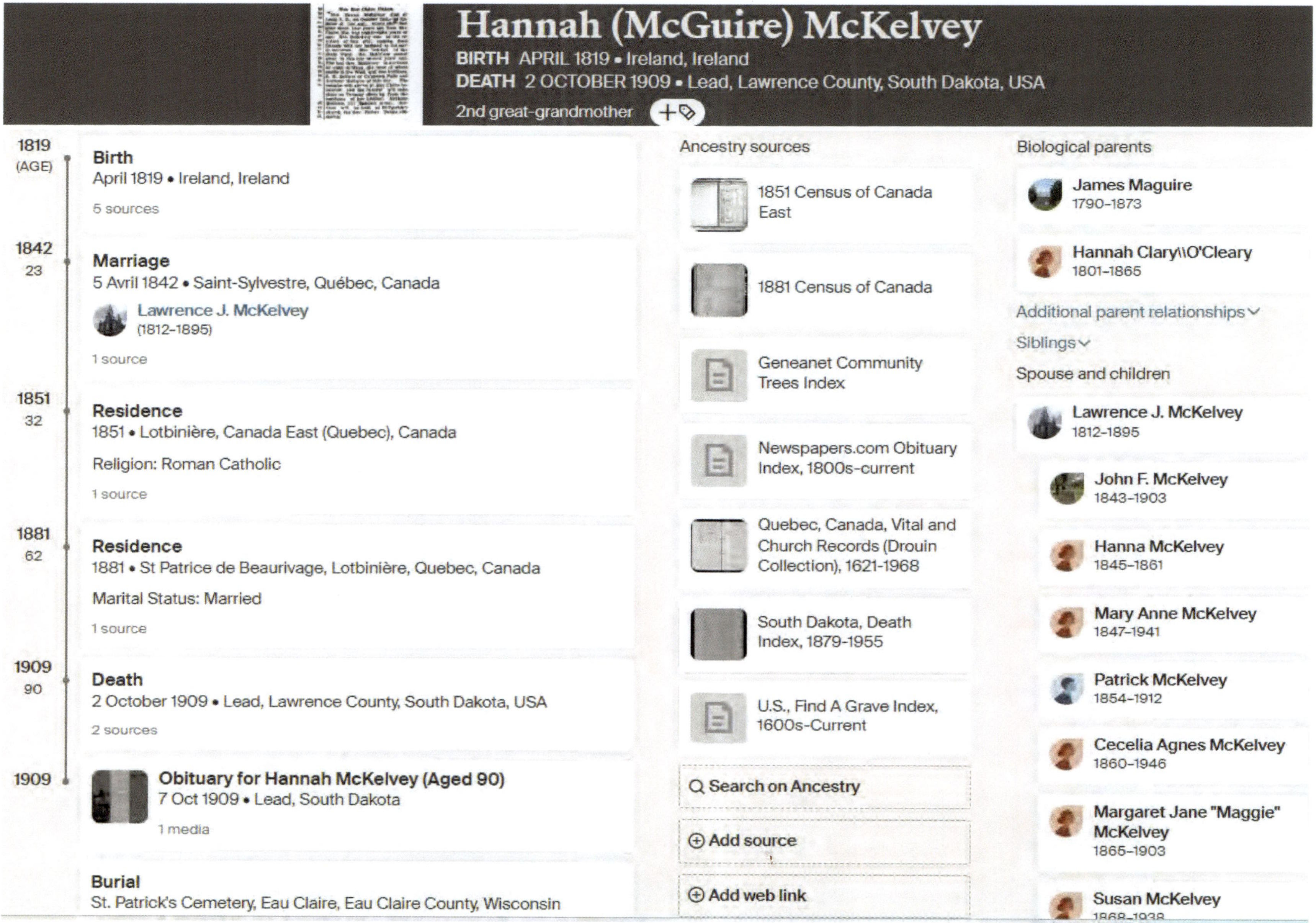

Hannah (McGuire) McKelvey

BIRTH APRIL 1819 • Ireland, Ireland
DEATH 2 OCTOBER 1909 • Lead, Lawrence County, South Dakota, USA
2nd great-grandmother

1819 (AGE)
Birth
April 1819 • Ireland, Ireland
5 sources

1842 23
Marriage
5 Avril 1842 • Saint-Sylvestre, Québec, Canada
Lawrence J. McKelvey (1812–1895)
1 source

1851 32
Residence
1851 • Lotbinière, Canada East (Quebec), Canada
Religion: Roman Catholic
1 source

1881 62
Residence
1881 • St Patrice de Beaurivage, Lotbinière, Quebec, Canada
Marital Status: Married
1 source

1909 90
Death
2 October 1909 • Lead, Lawrence County, South Dakota, USA
2 sources

1909
Obituary for Hannah McKelvey (Aged 90)
7 Oct 1909 • Lead, South Dakota
1 media

Burial
St. Patrick's Cemetery, Eau Claire, Eau Claire County, Wisconsin

Ancestry sources
- 1851 Census of Canada East
- 1881 Census of Canada
- Geneanet Community Trees Index
- Newspapers.com Obituary Index, 1800s-current
- Quebec, Canada, Vital and Church Records (Drouin Collection), 1621-1968
- South Dakota, Death Index, 1879-1955
- U.S., Find A Grave Index, 1600s-Current
- Search on Ancestry
- Add source
- Add web link

Biological parents
- **James Maguire** 1790–1873
- **Hannah Clary\\O'Cleary** 1801–1865

Additional parent relationships
Siblings
Spouse and children
- **Lawrence J. McKelvey** 1812–1895
- **John F. McKelvey** 1843–1903
- **Hanna McKelvey** 1845–1861
- **Mary Anne McKelvey** 1847–1941
- **Patrick McKelvey** 1854–1912
- **Cecelia Agnes McKelvey** 1860–1946
- **Margaret Jane "Maggie" McKelvey** 1865–1903
- **Susan McKelvey** 1868–1938

John F. McKelvey

BIRTH 23 OCTOBER 1843 • Saint-Sylvestre, Lotbinière, Quebec, Canada
DEATH 18 JULY 1903 • Alpena, Alpena County, Michigan
great-grandfather

1843 (AGE)

Birth
23 October 1843 • Saint-Sylvestre, Lotbinière, Quebec, Canada
6 sources

1843

Baptism
1843 • Saint-Sylvestre, Lotbinière, Quebec, Canada
1 source

1851 8

Residence
1851 • Saint-Sylvestre, Lotbinière, Quebec, Canada
Religion: Roman Catholic
1 source

1861 18

Residence
1861 • Saint-Sylvestre, Lotbinière, Quebec, Canada
Marital Status: Single

1870 26

Marriage
6 September 1870 • Saint-Sylvestre, Lotbinière, Quebec, Canada
Catherine (Monaghan) McKelvey
(1849–1928)
1 source

1870 27

Residence
1870 • West Eau Claire, Eau Claire County, Wisconsin
Residence Post Office: West Eau Claire
1 source

Ancestry sources

- 1851 Census of Canada East
- 1861 Census of Canada
- 1870 United States Federal Census
- 1880 United States Federal Census
- 1900 United States Federal Census
- Canadian Genealogy Index, 1600s-1900s
- Michigan, Death Records, 1867-1952
- Michigan, Deaths and Burials Index, 1867-1995

Parents

- **Lawrence J. McKelvey** 1812–1895
- **Hannah (McGuire) McKelvey** 1819–1909

Siblings

Spouse and children

- **Catherine (Monaghan) McKelvey** 1849–1928
  - **Lawrence Patrick McKelvey** 1869–1943
  - **Mary Katherine McKelvey** 1878–1932
  - **Catherine Agnes McKelvey** 1880–1943
  - **Elizabeth Cecilia McKelvey** 1882–1968
  - **John Michael McKelvey** 1885–1935

JOHN F. MCKELVEY (1843-1903), our maternal great-grandfather, CONTINUED

1871
28

Residence
1871 • Wolfestown, Wolfe, Quebec, Canada

1 source

1880
37

Residence
1880 • Eau Claire, Eau Claire County, Wisconsin

Marital Status: Married; Relation to Head: Self

1 source

1885
42

Residence
1885 • Eau Claire, Eau Claire County, Wisconsin

1 source

1900
57

Residence
1900 • Alpena Ward 2, Alpena County, Michigan

Marital Status: Married

1 source

1903
59

Death
18 July 1903 • Alpena, Alpena County, Michigan

2 sources

Burial
Holy Cross Cemetery, Alpena, Alpena County, Michigan

Quebec, Canada, Vital and Church Records (Drouin Collection), 1621-1968

Quebec, Canada, Vital and Church Records (Drouin Collection), 1621-1968

Quebec, Canada, Vital and Church Records (Drouin Collection), 1621-1968

U.S. City Directories, 1822-1995

U.S., Find A Grave Index, 1600s-Current

U.S., Social Security Applications and Claims Index, 1936-2007

Search on Ancestry

⊕ Add source

⊕ Add web link

Eva Clair McKelvey
1887–1974

Ethel Miriam McKelvey
1890–1970

Helen Juanita McKelvey
1892–1918

⊕ Add family

Catherine (Monaghan) McKelvey

BIRTH 25 FEBRUARY 1849 • Saint-Sylvestre, Lotbinière, Quebec, Canada
DEATH 30 AUGUST 1928 • Alpena, Alpena County, Michigan
great-grandmother

1849 (AGE)	**Birth** 25 February 1849 • Saint-Sylvestre, Lotbinière, Quebec, Canada 7 sources
1849	**Baptism** 1849 • Saint-Sylvestre, Québec, Canada 1 source
1851 (2)	**Residence** 1851 • Lotbinière, Canada East (Quebec), Canada Religion: Roman Catholic 1 source
1870 (21)	**Marriage** 6 September 1870 • Saint-Sylvestre, Lotbinière, Quebec, Canada John F. McKelvey (1843-1903)
1880 (31)	**Residence** 1880 • Eau Claire, Eau Claire, Wisconsin, USA Marital Status: Married; Relation to Head: Wife 1 source
1900 (51)	**Residence** 1900 • Alpena Ward 2, Alpena County, Michigan, USA Marital Status: Married; Relation to Head: Wife 1 source

Ancestry sources

- 1851 Census of Canada East
- 1880 United States Federal Census
- 1900 United States Federal Census
- 1910 United States Federal Census
- 1920 United States Federal Census
- Michigan, Death Records, 1867-1952
- Michigan, Deaths and Burials Index, 1867-1995
- Quebec, Canada, Vital and Church Records (Drouin Collection), 1621-1968

Parents

- Patrick Monaghan, 1818–1899
- Margeurite McDade, 1817–1898

Spouse and children

- John F. McKelvey, 1843–1903
  - Lawrence Patrick McKelvey, 1869–1943
  - Mary Katherine McKelvey, 1878–1932
  - Catherine Agnes McKelvey, 1880–1943
  - Elizabeth Cecilia McKelvey, 1882–1968
  - John Michael McKelvey, 1885–1935
  - Eva Clair McKelvey, 1887–1974

CATHERINE (MONAGHAN) MCKELVEY (1849-1928), our maternal great-grandmother, CONTINUED

1910 61

Residence
1910 • Alpena Ward 5, Alpena, Michigan, USA

Marital Status: Widowed; Relation to Head of House: Head

1 source

1920 71

Residence
1920 • Alpena Ward 2, Alpena, Michigan, USA

Marital Status: Widowed; Relation to Head: Mother-in-law

1 source

1928 79

Death
30 August 1928 • Alpena, Alpena County, Michigan

Catherine was buried in Holy Cross Cemetery in Alpena.

U.S., Find A Grave Index, 1600s-Current

U.S., World War I Draft Registration Cards, 1917-1918

Search on Ancestry

Add source

Add web link

Ethel Miriam McKelvey
1890–1970

Helen Juanita McKelvey
1892–1918

Add family

John Michael McKelvey

BIRTH 12 JANUARY, 1885 • Eau Claire, Eau Claire County, Wisconsin, USA
DEATH 22 MARCH 1935 • Stockton, San Joaquin County, California, USA

maternal grandfather

1885 (AGE)

Birth
12 January, 1885 • Eau Claire, Eau Claire County, Wisconsin, USA

7 sources

1885

Baptism
18 January, 1885 • St. Patricks Catholic Church, Eau Claire, Eau Claire County, Wisconsin, USA

Godparents: Francis Gregor and Mary Monaghan

1900 15

Residence
1900 • Alpena Ward 2, Alpena, Michigan, USA

Marital Status: Single; Relation to Head: Son

1 source

1905 20

Marriage
1905? • California?

No record located.

Josephine Estelle (Theobald) McKelvey
(1880-1937)

1910 25

Residence
1910 • San Francisco Assembly District 38, San Francisco County, California, USA

Marital Status: Married; Relation to Head of House: Head

1 source

1915 30

Residence
1915 • San Francisco, California, USA

1 source

Ancestry sources

- 1900 United States Federal Census
- 1910 United States Federal Census
- 1920 United States Federal Census
- 1930 United States Federal Census
- California, Death Index, 1905-1939
- Newspapers.com Obituary Index, 1800s-current
- U.S. City Directories, 1822-1995
- U.S., Find A Grave Index, 1600s-Current
- U.S., World War I Draft Registration Cards, 1917-

Parents

John F. McKelvey
1843-1903

Catherine (Monaghan) McKelvey
1849-1928

Siblings

Spouse and children

Josephine Estelle (Theobald) McKelvey
1880-1937

Helen J. (McKelvey) Kelly
1906-1981

⊕ Add family

JOHN MICHAEL MCKELVEY (1885-1935), our maternal grandfather, CONTINUED

1915 • San Francisco, California, USA

1 source

1918 33

Military
1918 • Truckee, Nevada County, California, USA

John registered for the WWI military draft on 12 September, 1918. See Draft Registration card, attached. We do not know if he served.

1920 35

Residence
1920 • Truckee, Nevada County, California, USA

John lived in Truckee, but Meadow Lake is listed on the 1920 and 1930 U.S. Federal Census because that is the name of Truckee's Census Enumeration District. The mining town of Meadow Lake was abandoned and had no permanent residents by 1892 .

1 source

1930 45

Residence
1930 • Truckee, Nevada County, California. See comment above about Meadow Lake.

Marital Status: Single; Relation to Head: Brother.

1 source

1935 50

Death of John Michael McKelvey
22 March 1935 • Stockton, San Joaquin County, California

Death - obituary

1 media

1935 50

Death
22 March 1935 • Stockton, San Joaquin County, California, USA

1935

Burial
25 March, 1935 • St. Mary's Cemetery, Sacramento, Sacramento County, California, USA

1 source

U.S., World War I Draft Registration Cards, 1917-1918

Wisconsin, Births and Christenings Index, 1801-1928

Search on Ancestry

Add source

Add web link

Josephine Estelle (Theobald) McKelvey

BIRTH 7 JULY 1880 • Elk Grove, Sacramento County, California, USA
DEATH 20 NOV 1937 • San Francisco, California, USA

maternal grandmother

1880 (AGE)

Birth
7 July 1880 • Elk Grove, Sacramento County, California, USA

4 sources

1898 17

Marriage
11 January, 1898 • Fairfield, Solano County, California, USA

William W. Conner

1 source

1900 20

Residence
1900 • Sacramento, Sacramento County, California, USA

Marital Status: Married; Relation to Head: Wife

1 source

1905 25

Marriage
1905? • California?

No record located.

John Michael McKelvey (1885–1935)

1910 30

Residence
1910 • San Francisco Assembly District 38, San Francisco County, California, USA

Marital Status: Married; Relation to Head of House: Wife

1 source

Ancestry sources

- 1900 United States Federal Census
- 1910 United States Federal Census
- 1920 United States Federal Census
- 1930 United States Federal Census
- California, County Birth, Marriage, and Death Records, 1849-1980
- California, Death Index, 1905-1939
- California, San Francisco Area Funeral Home Records, 1895-1985
- U.S. City Directories, 1822-1995

Parents

- **Joseph Paxton Theobald** 1847–1910
- **Mary Louise (Wilts) Theobald** 1856–1931

Spouse and children

- **William W. Conner**
  - **James David Conner** 1898–1977
  - **Gertrude (Conner) Reubold** 1902–1981

Spouse and children

- **John Michael McKelvey** 1885–1935
  - **Helen J. (McKelvey) Kelly** 1906–1981

Spouse

- **Roy Decker** 1889–

JOSEPHINE (THEOBALD) MCKELVEY (1880-1937), our maternal grandmother, CONTINUED

1915
35

Residence
1915 • San Francisco, California, USA

1 source

1920
40

Residence
1920 • San Francisco Assembly District 30, San Francisco County California, USA

Marital Status: Widowed; Relation to Head: Head

1 source

1937
57

Death
20 November 1937 • San Francisco, San Francisco County, California, USA

1 source

⊕ Add source

⊕ Add web link

Helen J. (McKelvey) Kelly

BIRTH 9 AUGUST 1906 • Truckee, Nevada County, California, USA
DEATH 14 AUGUST 1981 • Santa Cruz, Santa Cruz County, California, USA

1906
(AGE)

Birth
9 August 1906 • Truckee, Nevada County, California, USA

Helen may have been named after one of her father John's younger sisters, Helen Juanita McKelvey, who was 16 years old when Helen June was born.

6 sources

1910
4

Residence
1910 • San Francisco Assembly District 38, San Francisco County, California, USA

Marital Status: Single; Relation to Head of House: Daughter

1 source

1920
14

Residence
1920 • San Francisco Assembly District 30, San Francisco County, California, USA

Marital Status: Single; Relation to Head: Daughter

1 source

1943
37

Marriage
29 Aug 1943 • Santa Cruz, California, USA
Joseph Lester Kelly
(1895–1967)

1 source 1 media

Ancestry sources

- 1910 United States Federal Census
- 1920 United States Federal Census
- 1950 United States Federal Census
- California, Death Index, 1940-1997
- Newspapers.com Marriage Index, 1800s-1999
- U.S., Find A Grave Index, 1600s-Current
- U.S., Social Security Death Index, 1935-2014

Parents

John Michael McKelvey
1885–1935

Josephine Estelle (Theobald) McKelvey
1880–1937

Siblings

Spouse and children

Joseph Lester Kelly
1895–1967

Joyce Vivian Kelly
1944–

James David Kelly
1945–

Katherine Elizabeth Kelly
1947–

Julie (Kelly) DiMaggio
1947–

Spouse

HELEN J. (MCKELVEY) KELLY (1906-1981), MOTHER, CONTINUED

1943
37

Residence
Abt 1943 • Oakland

1 source

1950
44

Residence
1950 • Oakland, Alameda, California, USA

Relation to Head: Wife; Marital Status: Married

1 source

1981
75

Death
14 August 1981 • Santa Cruz, Santa Cruz County, California, USA

3 sources

Burial
Colma, San Mateo County, California, USA

1 source

Search on Ancestry

⊕ Add source

⊕ Add web link

William McNally

⊕ Add family

Appendix Two

Origins within County Donegal of our Direct McKelvey Ancestors

Canadian and U. S. records show that our earliest identified direct McKelvey ancestors (our 3x and 2x great-grandparents) were born in County Donegal. Identifying their locations **within** the County might reveal earlier ancestors and insights into their lives.

Find-a-Grave records for John McKelvey and for Hanna McGuire's **parents** show their birthplaces as "Donegal, County Donegal" and "Ballyshannon, County Donegal" respectively (see page 45). However, information displayed on Find-a-Grave is secondary (reported long after death) and we have no similar information on the origins within County Donegal of Mary Ellen (Slevin) McKelvey and Lawrence McKelvey. This Appendix displays analyses supporting **tentative** identification of the civil parish[38] origins of the first two generations of our direct McKelvey ancestors.

First Two Generations of Direct McKelvey Ancestors

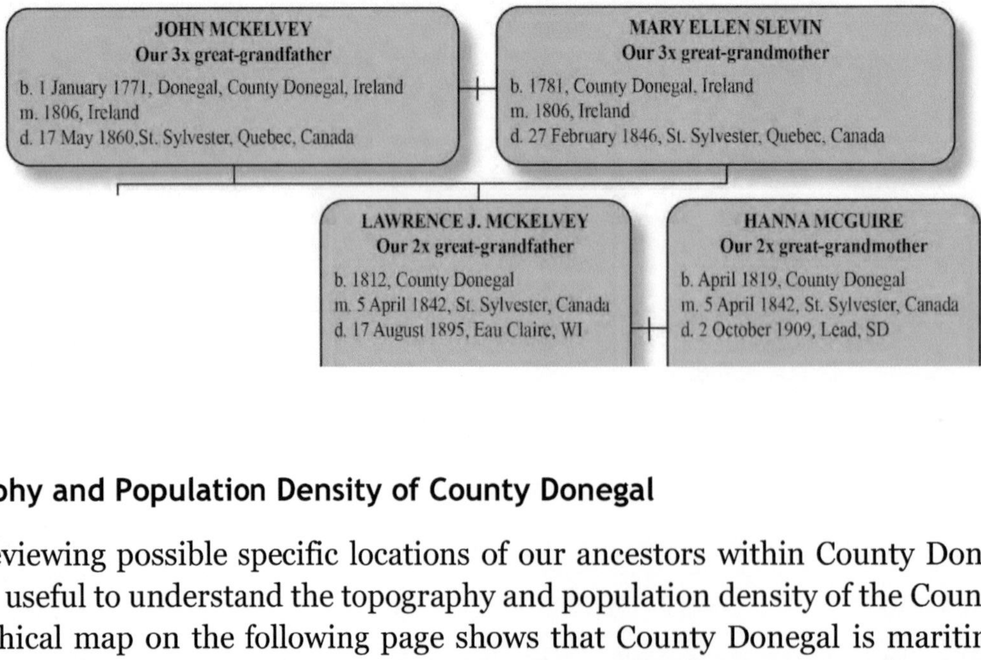

Topography and Population Density of County Donegal

Before reviewing possible specific locations of our ancestors within County Donegal, it would be useful to understand the topography and population density of the County. The topographical map on the following page shows that County Donegal is maritime and mountainous with fertile farmland in the eastern part of the County, near the border with Northern Ireland. This suggests that fishing families would cluster along the coast, while farmers, like our McKelveys, would cluster in and north of the Finn Valley and Lifford.

[38] Ireland has Catholic parishes and Protestant Church of Ireland (civil) parishes. Britain's administrative records, like Griffith's Valuation (discussed below), were organized by civil parish.

County Donegal Topography with the Finn Valley Area, Donegal Town, and Ballyshannon

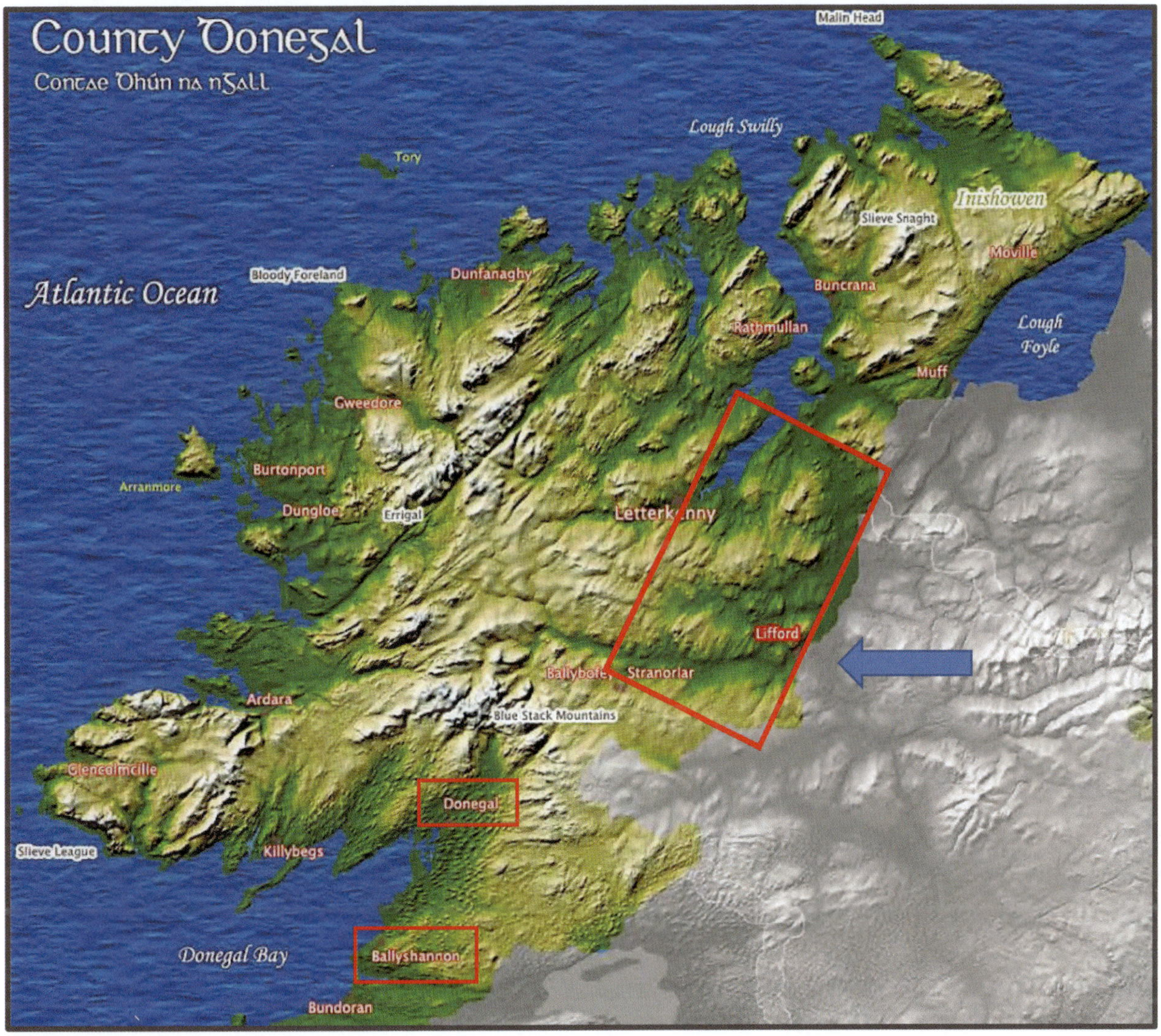

The green valley of the River Finn, marked by the blue arrow, flows east to west. The Finn Valley Area also includes the fertile green area north of Lifford.

I could not locate a population density map for 19th-century Ireland. But I did locate the map below showing the density in 2006. County Donegal is rural and lightly populated, with a 2006 population of 147, 264 which is very similar to its 1831 population of 141,845 according to Ireland's Central Statistical Office.

Therefore, it's likely that the 2006 population density of County Donegal approximates its 19th-century population density. Based on availability of fertile farmland and estimated 19th-century population density, the McKelveys may have originated in the fertile farming area marked by the large red rectangles above and on the County Donegal density map on the following page. Donegal Town and Ballyshannon also are candidates for origins based on Find-a-Grave data displayed page 45.

Population Density of Ireland (left) and Detail of County Donegal (right), 2006
Irish Ordnance Survey Data

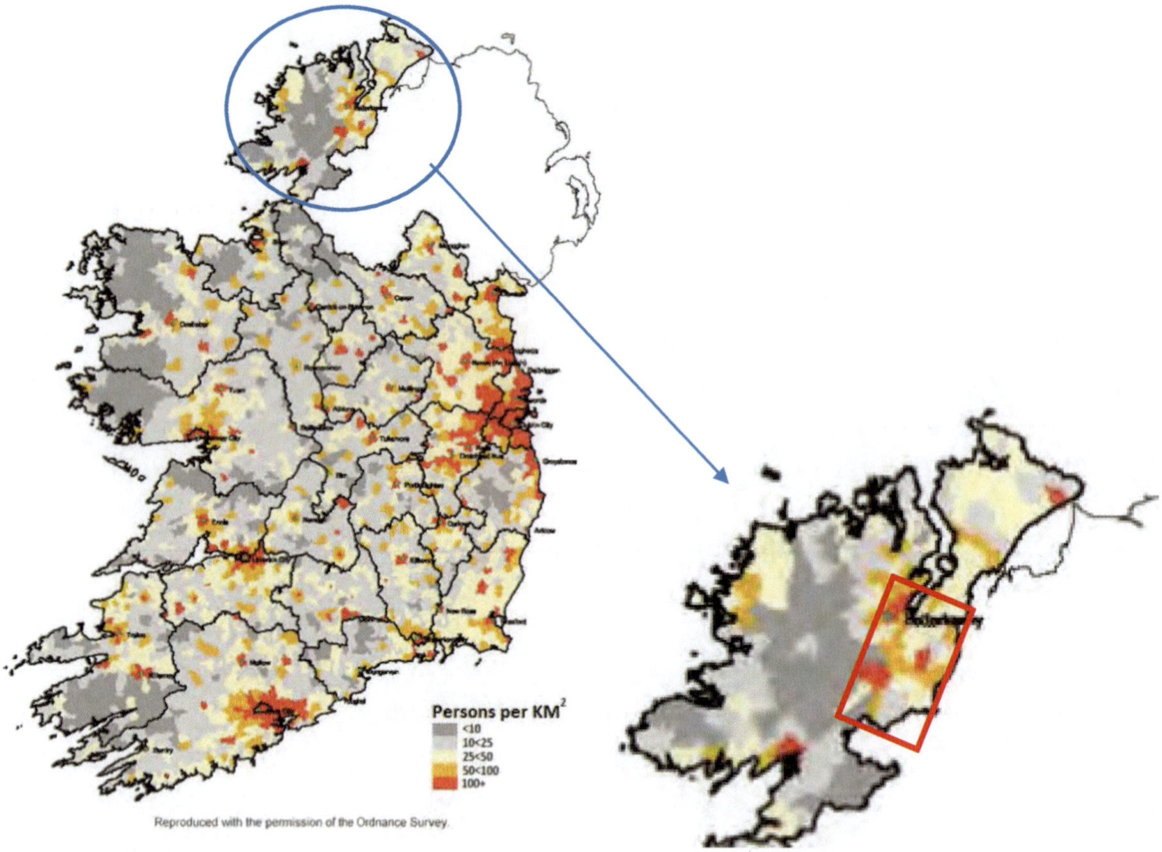

Data Sources: Find-a-Grave

Next, we will turn to 19th-century data to learn where our direct McKelvey ancestors born in County Donegal–the McKelveys, Slevins, and McGuires–may have lived within the County before immigrating to Canada in 1832-36. There are few public data sources to identify specific parish and townland locations of early 19th-century residents of Ireland, due to records being destroyed or not collected.[39] In the absence of 19th-century population records, genealogists turn to Find-a-Grave and two 19th-century land surveys–the Tithe Applotment and Griffith's Valuation.[40]

---

[39] Reasons for missing 19th century and earlier Irish records are listed on page 9 above.

[40] Find-a-Grave dates and locations are secondary data, requiring additional data for verification. In contrast, Tithe Applotment and Griffith's Valuation are primary data and therefore more reliable. However, Find-a-Grave records can be linked to ancestors if birth and death dates and locations correspond to data from other sources. Land surveys have other problems, discussed below.

Find-a-Grave records include dates and locations of people's births and deaths. Birth locations, shown below, are for our direct McKelvey ancestors who were born in Ireland.

Direct Ancestors born in Ireland	Location of Birth on Find-A-Grave
John McKelvey (1771-1860)	Donegal, County Donegal
Mary Ellen (Slevin) McKelvey (1781-1846)	County Donegal
Lawrence McKelvey (1812-1895)	County Donegal
Hanna McGuire (1819-1909)	No location for Hanna (b. 1819), but her parents-James and Hannah-were born in Ballyshannon, Co. Donegal.

Name:	John McKelvey
Gender:	Male
Birth Date:	1 Jan 1771
Birth Place:	Donegal, County Donegal, Ireland
Death Date:	17 May 1860
Death Place:	Saint-Sylvestre, Chaudiere-Appalaches Region, Quebec, Canada
Cemetery:	Saint Sylvestre Cemetery
mation Place:	Saint-Sylvestre, Chaudiere-Appalaches Region, Quebec, Canada
Has Bio?:	N
Spouse:	Mary McKelvey
Children:	Catherine McKelvey
URL:	https://www.findagrave.com/memorial/136856272/john-mckelvey

Name:	James Maguire
Birth Date:	1791
Birth Place:	Ballyshannon, County Donegal, Ireland
Death Date:	29 Dec 1873
Death Place:	Saint-Gilles, Chaudiere-Appalaches Region, Quebec, Canada
Cemetery:	Saint Sylvestre Cemetery
mation Place:	Saint-Sylvestre, Chaudiere-Appalaches Region, Quebec, Canada
Has Bio?:	N
Spouse:	Hannah Maguire
URL:	https://www.findagrave.com/memorial/137284428/james-maguire

Name:	Hannah Maguire
Birth Date:	1795
Birth Place:	Ballyshannon, County Donegal, Ireland
Death Date:	1865
Death Place:	Saint-Gilles, Chaudiere-Appalaches Region, Quebec, Canada
Cemetery:	Saint Sylvestre Cemetery
mation Place:	Saint-Sylvestre, Chaudiere-Appalaches Region, Quebec, Canada
Has Bio?:	N
Spouse:	James Maguire
URL:	https://www.findagrave.com/memorial/137049965/hannah-maguire

Find-a-Grave shows that John McKelvey was born in "Donegal," but does not specify Donegal "Town." Hanna McGuire's **parents** were born in Ballyshannon Townland.

Data Sources: 19th-Century Land Surveys

Land surveys conducted by the English to tax Irish farmers produce primary data, but they are not ideal for genealogical research because they list "principal occupiers" or heads of families, not entire families. Also, they do not include birth dates and birth locations of occupiers. Therefore, additional facts (e.g., from cluster analyses, displayed below) are required to distinguish our ancestors from others with the same name.

Nonetheless, land records can be useful for genealogical research because Irish families tended to remain in or near the same geographic areas as their Gaelic ancestors. Also, children in farming families tended to marry neighbors who may be distant cousins. Thus, parents, siblings, cousins, and other relatives may be listed on a land survey conducted several decades after our ancestors immigrated.

Historian and genealogist Edward MacLysagh (1857-1986) described this tradition:

> One of the most striking phenomena . . . is the tenacity of families to have continued dwelling for centuries, down to the present day, in the very districts where their names originated. This obtains in almost every county in Ireland . . . The extent to which present-day descendants of the old Gaelic families still inhabit the territories occupied by the medieval septs from which they stem is most remarkable. **Source**: *Tracing our Donegal Ancestors* by Helen Meehan and Godfrey Duffy, Flyleaf Press, 2014, page 104.

Many genealogists have told me that their 19th-century, and earlier, Irish ancestors married neighbors who lived within a half-hour walk of their farms.

Analysis of Griffith's Valuation (GV) Records with Genealogy Clustering

The geographic stability of Irish families means that analyzing locations of "FAN (family, associates, and neighbor) clusters"[41] might identify and possibly validate the geographic origins of our McKelvey ancestors. The most complete land survey[42] of 19th-century Ireland is Griffith's Valuation (GV) of c. 1857.[43] Like other land surveys, GV recorded the names of the principal "occupiers" (heads of families)[44] of land in civil (Church of Ireland) parishes and townlands, the smallest administrative land unit.

Surname variants

Before analyzing records, we need to identify all reasonable surname variants of our ancestors because they were illiterate and depended on others to record their names. Consequently, our ancestors may have been recorded under several different surnames. John Grenham's website (www.johngrenham.com) is the most comprehensive source of GV surname variants. Grenham identified the following surname variants for our four earliest identified direct ancestors in County Donegal–McKelvey, McKelvy, Slevin, McGuire, and Maguire–as GV "occupiers" (heads of households/families).[45]

---

[41] FAN cluster analysis uses data, e.g., land records, to research something, e.g., location of a group of family members, associates, and/or neighbors. The following site links to many articles and YouTube presentations on FAN cluster analysis: https://www.cyndislist.com/research-methodology/fan-club/#:~:text=It%20refers%20to%20researching%20everyone,(s)%20surrounding%20your%20ancestor.

[42] An earlier land survey, the Tithe Applotment (TA) was conducted in 1834. This Survey might have been helpful for identifying our McKelveys who emigrated between 1834-1836. However, the TA is far from complete. For example, 79 distinct Slevin families are listed on GV compared to only 11 on TA.

[43] The English conducted GV in County Donegal in 1857, about 20 years after the McKelveys left.

[44] At that time, a typical family consisted of 7 people. Therefore, each occupier represents 7 people.

[45] Grenham also corrects for overcounting unique individuals on GV because one person may occupy multiple plots. Grenham omits all entries without a house. Thus, he lists 6 McKelveys in Stranorlar, rather than 10, because 4 of them had no house on their land. See www.johngrenham.com.

Locations of McKelvey, McKelvy, Slevin, McGuire, and Maguire GV Occupiers, 1857

Family cluster analyses of GV data confirm three **areas** in County Donegal—the Finn Valley, Donegal Town, and Ballyshannon Township—as the most likely locations of our McKelvey family ancestors. These areas and their civil parishes are analyzed below

Donegal Town, Ballyshannon Township, and the Finn Valley Area between Ballybofey and Raphoe

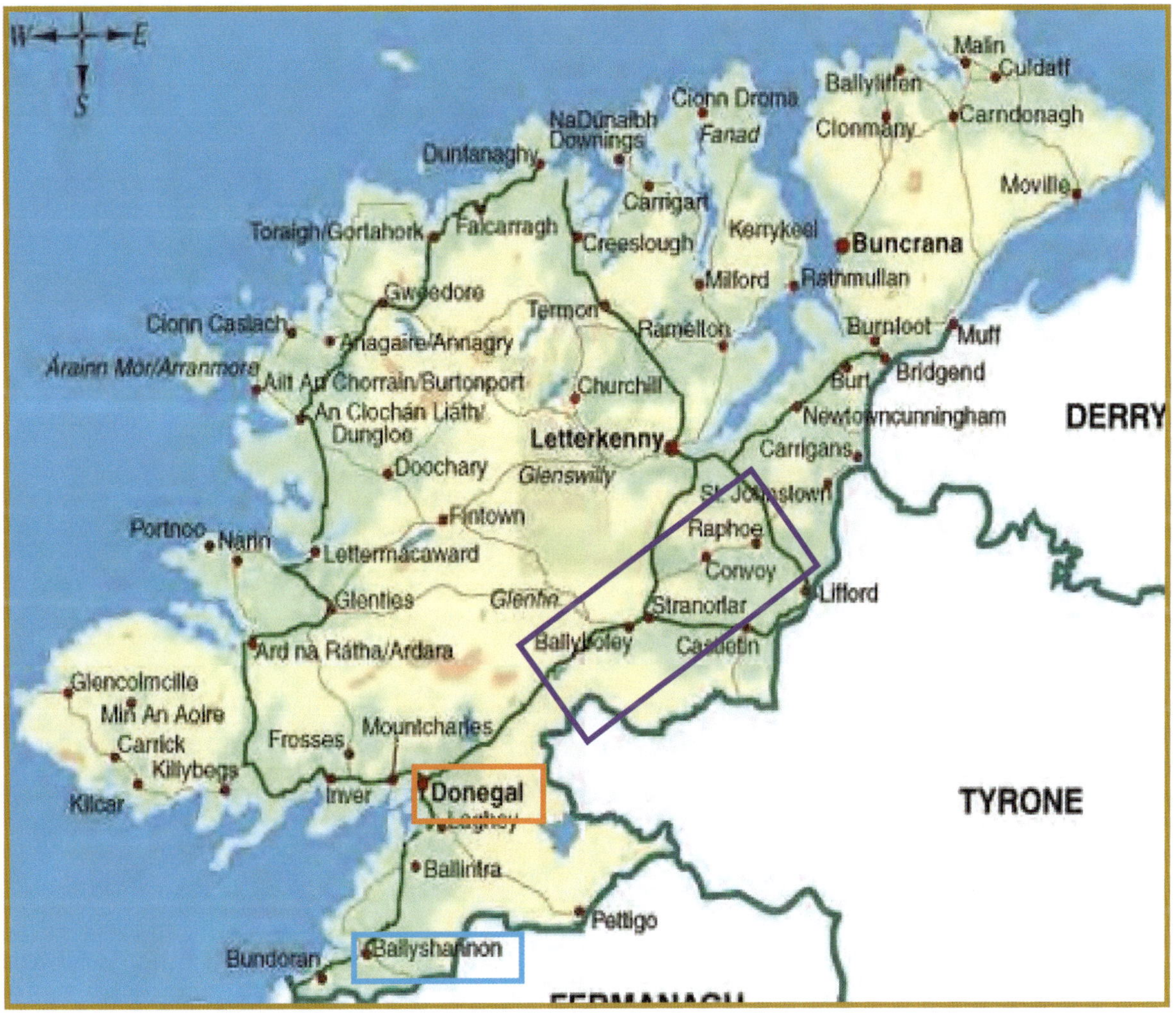

Yellow areas are mountains; mountain peaks are tan; and farming areas are light green. The distance between Ballybofey and Raphoe is 22 km or 14 miles.

The tables and maps below display civil parish locations of GV occupiers in three areas–the Finn Valley (in and north of the River Finn Valley), Donegal Town, and Ballyshannon Townland. The tables list all occupiers. The maps display civil parishes with two or more ancestral surnames.

FINN VALLEY AREA

Surname Variants, Civil Parish Names and Identification Numbers, and Number of Occupier Families in Each Civil Parish, GV, 1857

McKelvey*	McKelvy	Slevin*	McGuire*	Maguire
8 in Co. Donegal	26 in Co.Donegal	72 in County Donegal	59 in Co. Donegal	62 in Co. Donegal
7 in Finn Valley	11 in Finn Valley	28 in Finn Valley	6 in Finn Valley	6 in Finn Valley
Convoy (11) 1	Convoy (11) 3	Convoy (11) 3	Convoy (11) 1	--
--	Raphoe (43) 1	Raphoe (43) 1	Raphoe (43) 1	--
Stranorlar (46) 6	--	Stranorlar (46) 1	--	--
--	Donaghmore (16) 5	Donaghmore (16) 13	Donaghmore (16) 1	Donaghmore (16) 4
--	Leck (37) 2	--	Leck (37) 4	--
--	--	Clonleigh (9) 1	--	--
--	--	Killteevoge (32) 9	--	Killteevoge (32) 2

Civil parish names are from John Grenham's portal to GV data. But the identification numbers (in parentheses) are from an Ulster Historical Foundation map, shown below and on the next page.

*The spelling variants—McKelvey, Slevin, and McGuire—in this Family History reflect frequency on Canadian and U.S. records of our ancestors, although I have seen other variants in those records.

Source: John Grenham's portal to GV data at https://www.askaboutireland.ie/griffith-valuation/

Two civil parishes (11 and 16) have four surnames, 1 civil parishes (43) has 3 ancestral surnames, and 3 civil parishes (32, 37, and 46) have 2 ancestral surnames

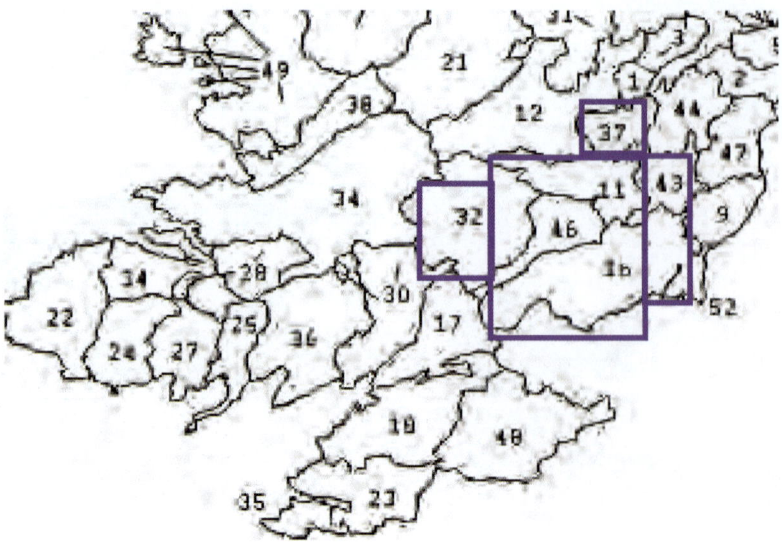

DONEGAL TOWN AND BALLYSHANNON TOWNSHIP AREAS

Surname Variants, Names and Identification Numbers of Civil Parishes, and Number of Occupier Families in Each Civil Parish, GV, 1857

Area of County Donegal	McKelvey 8 in Co. Donegal 1 in Donegal Town 0 in Ballyshannon	McKelvy 26 in Co. Donegal 4 in Donegal Town 0 in Ballyshannon	Slevin 72 in Co. Donegal 27 in Donegal Town 15 in Ballyshannon	McGuire* 59 in Co. Donegal 1 in Donegal Twn 4 in Ballyshannon	Maguire* 62 in Co. Donegal 30 in Donegal Town 17 in Ballyshannon
Donegal Town	Killymard (30) 1 -- --	Killymard (30) 1 -- Invert (36) 3	Killymard (30) 3 Donegal (17) 20 Inver (36) 4	-- -- Inver (36) 1	Killymard (30) 3 Donegal (17) 1 Inver (36) 26
Ballyshannon	-- --	-- --	Kilbarron (23) 13 Inishmacsaint (35) 2	Kilbarron (23) 2 Inishmacsaint (35) 2	Kilbarron (23) 8 Inishmacsaint (35) 9
Carryover Finn Valley	7	11	28	7	6
Other Areas of Co. Donegal	0	11	2	47	9

See the notes below the Finn Valley table on the previous page.

Two civil parishes near Donegal Town (30 and 36) have 4 ancestral surnames. Donegal Parish (17) has 2 ancestral names. Two civil parishes near Ballyshannon (23 and 35) have 3 ancestral surnames.

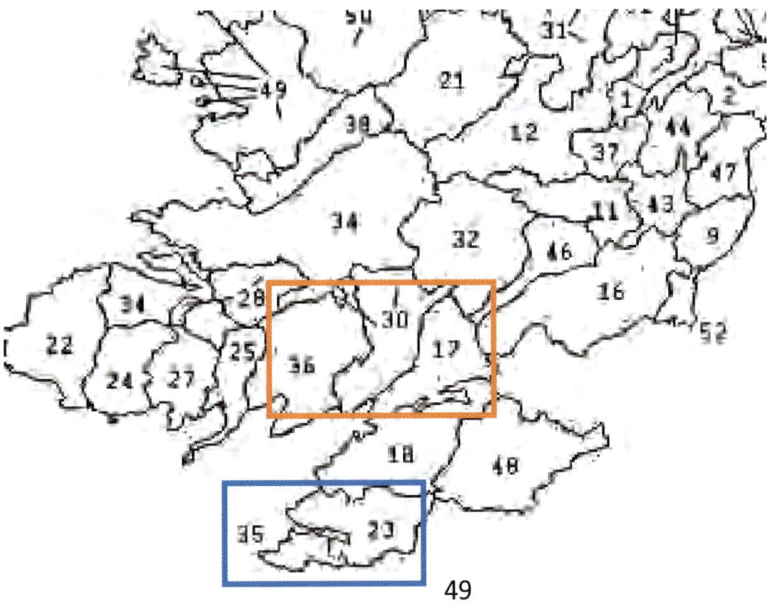

Summary

To identify the specific origins within County Donegal of our earliest direct McKelvey ancestors, I entered each of their five most common surnames (McKelvey/McKelvy, Slevin, and McGuire /Maguire) into John Grenham's portal to access 1857 Griffith's Valuation land surveys. I hoped to identify civil parishes with multiple ancestral surnames and then drill down to specific townlands (Ireland's smallest jurisdiction) within civil parishes with more than one surname.

The tables and maps on the prior two pages show that 11 civil parishes, among 52 in County Donegal, had 2 or more of the 5 surnames listed above. These are: 6 parishes in the Finn Valley Area; 3 parishes near Donegal Town; and 2 parishes in the Ballyshannon Area. (The names of these parishes are listed in the tables above). but no townlands within those parishes had more than one of the five ancestral surnames. Therefore, I could not identify townlands and parishes of origin and instead, concluded that our ancestors likely originated in one or more of three areas: (1) in and north of the Finn Valley; (2) near Donegal Town; and (3) near Ballyshannon.

Finn Valley

Donegal Town

Ballyshannon

Appendix Three

Jim's 2019 emails from County Donegal

Jim began researching our Irish ancestors in 2018 while preparing for a 2019 genealogical research trip to Ireland with his wife Robin. Using Ancestry.com and LDS' FamilySearch websites, Jim traced our McKelvey line from California back to Michigan, Wisconsin, Quebec, and finally to County Donegal in Ireland. Our 3x and 2x great-grandfathers, John and Lawrence McKelvey, were born in County Donegal.

Genealogical websites identified the county but not the townland or parish of our earliest identified McKelvey ancestors. But on FamilySearch, Jim identified several McKelveys, including a John McKelvey, in Ballybofey on the Griffiths Valuation land survey (see **Appendix Two**). Therefore, Jim and Robin added Ballybofey to their itinerary, hoping to identify our ancestors from local records not available elsewhere. Other records showed that a John McKelvey of Ballybofey was charged with theft and fighting beginning in 1859, but this occurred after our John McKelvey emigrated.[46]

Jim's emails by date

12 July 2019: Tomorrow, we head to Donegal, the site of the prodigal McKelvey clan. I pulled up some old court records for John McKelvey, who was very well-known to the local constabulary, both for minor civil and criminal matters.

14 July 2019: Another day of magnificent scenery! We left Connemara Sands Hotel and drove to Ballybofey in County Donegal, about 225 kms. Ballybofey is the city where John McKelvey lived. (*Note from Joyce*: John McKelveys lived in several other locations in County Donegal. See Appendix Two). From LDS records, he was a bit of a scoundrel, as he appeared several times in the Petty Sessions Court on several occasions with civil squabbles and minor criminal matters. (*Note from Joyce*: see footnote 49 below). He had to have been prosperous since he owned land and emigrated with his entire family.

Scenery today ran the gamut, from wild North Atlantic shoreline, beautiful fjords, lakes, and rivers, and, of course, the stacked stone fences and magnificent stone houses, most in great shape but some crumbling. The weather was perfect, with air temperatures in the mid-high 70's, and mostly sunny with no wind. Ballybofey (pronounced Bally bow FAY) is hosting a Gaelic football tournament today, so the town is packed. We just walked around and it's another charming little city. Since govt is closed today, we dropped into

[46] ***Note from Joyce***: We know that this John McKelvey was not our 3x great-grandfather and was not married to Mary Slaven, because our John McKelvey immigrated to Canada before 1837.

a small store and asked the young female clerk about historical records for the area. She didn't miss a beat, but just said, pointing to the back of the store: Oh, go ask Joe, he knows everything!

Joe turned out to be a helpful guy in his 50's, maybe the store manager, who directed us to the Ballybofey & Stranorlar District Historical Society, which is nearby and opens tomorrow. He also pointed us to an insurance company office near his store to speak to the owner, Caramel McKelvey, who is supposed to know lots about the local McKelveys. So, we have a thread we will try to follow.

I have found that the tales of helpful Irish people who enjoy helping expat Irish are true. We have not met one person who was curt or rude when asked for directions or local info. Instead, they are polite, helpful, and curious about who we are, where we come from, and what we're doing. The accents are really strong out in the country, though they seem to understand me better than I understand them.

15 July 2019: I had high hopes for investigating the McKelvey connections in Ballybofey, Donegal, but nothing came of them. I wasn't able to contact locals Caramel McKelvey or Pat McKelvey in Ballybofey, as both were out of town. Maybe locals leave town when it hosts a big sporting match, like the Gaelic football tournament.

We did go to the local records depository in the admin office of St. Joseph's Hospital in Ballybofey, which is associated with St. Joseph's Church. We spent about an hour with Marie Greene, a local clerk who handles genealogy among other admin duties. She was delighted to tell us what she knew. Unfortunately, their records only go back as far as 1860, almost 30 years after John McKelvey left Ireland with family for Canada. I showed her the Griffiths Valuation records for McKelveys for local townlands, but nothing stood out for her. According to her, there are no records anywhere, including church and parish records, that go back to 1771, when John McKelvey was born. (*Note from Joyce*–this is consistent with information provided by genealogists I contacted.)

What I hoped to find was John McKelvey's birth certificate, or even a marriage certificate, either of which may show his parents. Unfortunately, it was not to be. I am beginning to think that, when the records dry up with a certain generation, such as John McKelvey, it's not because someone lost interest in the research, it's because further records don't exist. Of course, that designation of information as difficult to find only makes the OCD researcher in all of us more determined.

We have driven south today, with occasional side trips toward the ocean. There are isolated remnants of stone homes, buildings, and fortresses, some with stone turrets overlooking the ocean, which must have been lookouts for early detection of invaders.

Jim and Robin at home in Fiji

Wild Atlantic Way in County Donegal

McKelvey's Bar in Ballybofey hosts outstanding Traditional Music Sessions

Contemporary photo of Ballybofey

Appendix Four

Reasons for Irish Emigration before the Great Hunger of 1845-1852

This essay summarizes the economic, political, and religious restrictions that prompted Irish tenant farmers to emigrate from the 1700s until the early 20th century.

England Defeated Ireland and Awarded Native Catholics' Land to Anglicans

For generations, the Irish owned and farmed their ancestors' land. But, in 1171, Henry II of England seized control of Ireland and took the title "Lord of Ireland." Anglo-Normans (the medieval ruling class of England, following the Norman conquest) gradually conquered Irish land which the King claimed. After a failed Irish rebellion in 1542, Henry VIII tightened England's control over Ireland. Gaelic Ireland was defeated and Ireland became part of the British Empire after the battle of Kinsale in 1601. After each English invasion of Ireland, the conquerors claimed and awarded Irish land to English gentry and soldiers.

Henry VIII also broke with the Roman Catholic Church and created the Church of England, resulting in the rise of Protestantism across England, Scotland, and Wales. Ireland resisted Protestantism, and when England failed to force it upon the Irish, King James I (1566-1625) created "Plantations" in Ireland, beginning in the 17th century. Plantations were a scheme developed by King James to replace the landowning Irish Catholic ruling class by seizing and awarding their land (ranging from dozens to thousands of acres) to loyal Anglican English and Scottish colonists.[47]

Like much of the rest of Europe, land in Ireland was the main source of political power, social prestige, and economic development. Landlords were the political elite in Ireland until national independence. By the mid-nineteenth century, most of Ireland was in the hands of 8,000 to 10,000 English and Scottish Anglican landowners, and fewer than 1,000 of these owned more than 50% of the land.[48] By the mid-19th century, 97% of Irish farmers were tenants, leasing land from British and Anglo-Irish landowners.[49]

---

[47] Descendants of Ulster Scotch Protestant settlers emigrated to North America during the 19th century to escape sectarian violence. In general, Catholics fought for independence from Britain, while Protestants fought against independence. Violence continued until the Good Friday Agreement of 1998.

[48] Irish farmers regained ownership of their land beginning in 1903 with passage of the Wyndham Land Act, providing low-cost government loans. By 1914, 80% of Irish tenants had purchased their holdings.

[49] The McKelveys and their spouses likely farmed land on or near their ancestors' farmlands.

Most landowners in Ireland hired managers to collect rents and oversee their estates because landlords preferred to live in England. Some managers treated Irish farmers well, but many extracted exorbitant rents and evicted tenants who improved their cottages and land. Throughout the 18th and 19th centuries, as the Irish population rapidly grew, farmers subdivided their farms among their children. By the mid-19th century, most Irish farms had become too small to support more than one family.

The Penal Laws of 1695-1829

Religious Penal Laws also motivated Irish Catholics to emigrate. England enacted Penal Laws in 1695 to force Irish Catholics to convert to Anglicanism by denying the rights of the native Catholic majority. Unless they converted, Irish Catholics would remain sharecropping farmers.[50] The Penal Laws made it illegal for Catholics to send their children to school; own land, a business, or property; practice their religion; hunt or fish; vote; or hold public office. The Laws also banned Irish culture, music, and education. Most Penal Laws were removed between 1778 and 1793. In 1829, the remaining Penal Laws were revoked.

Irish rebellions, especially in Ulster between Catholics and Protestants

Conflicts intensified between a Protestant landholding minority and a growing Catholic majority since England first invaded Ireland in the 12th century. The Irish Rebellion of 1798 was the most concentrated episode of violence up to that time. Seeking to prevent the Irish from destabilizing Britain or providing a base for foreign invasion, England passed an Act of Union in 1800 that made Ireland part of England and abolished the Irish Parliament. After many Irish Catholics opposed the Union, Britain enacted the Roman Catholic Relief Act in 1829, repealing many anti-Catholic laws, including remaining Penal Laws, and allowing Catholics into the English Parliament.

Daniel O'Connell (1775-1847), the first Catholic MP since 1689, unsuccessfully fought to repeal the Act of Union and restore Irish-self-government. O'Connell's tactics were largely peaceful, however, sporadic violence continued. The most sustained outbreak of violence was the Tithe War of the 1830s, over the obligation of Catholic farmers to pay tithes to the Protestant Church of Ireland. Meanwhile, in Ulster, there were repeated outbreaks of sectarian violence between Catholics and the growing Protestant Orange Order, likely contributing to the McKelveys' decision to emigrate.

---

[50] To maintain their land and rights, many landowning Irish Catholics converted to Anglicanism, robbing Irish Catholic tenant farmers of the leadership of the educated, landowning class.

Inability to Improve Conditions for their Families

During the 17th and 18th centuries, farmers throughout Ireland barely survived on potatoes while paying rent to Protestant landlords and tithes to the Church of Ireland. The Napoleonic Wars contributed to a brief period of relative prosperity, but by 1822, Ireland suffered famine, inflation, and the end of war-induced prosperity. The McKelveys emigrated between 1832 and 1836, along with one million other Irish who left during the century preceding the Great Hunger (*An Gorta Mór*) of 1845-1852.[51]

During and after the Great Hunger, emigration increased. Between 1841 and 1911, Ireland's population decreased by 46%, from 8.18 to 4.38 million. In addition to the one million people who died of starvation and related diseases during the Great Hunger, three million–primarily between the ages of 15 and 30–left Ireland to seek better lives elsewhere. The high rate of Irish emigration was unequaled in any other country, reflecting the lack of prospects for all but wealthy Irish landowners, and the demand for immigrant labor in the U.S., Canada, and England.

19th-century Irish Farmers Harvesting with Scythes

[51] Historians refer to "hunger" (rather than "famine") because the English government used the principle of a "free market" to justify the continued exportation of food from Ireland to Britain, while Irish farmers' only food (the potato crop) failed repeatedly.

Appendix Five

19th-Century Quebec: Irish Immigrant Life and our McKelveys' Villages

This Appendix includes essays on three aspects of the lives of Irish farmers who immigrated to Quebec during the mid-19th century: (1) advice to emigrants, distributed in Ireland and at the Port of Quebec; (2) Irish Canadian Catholicism; and (3) the development of an Irish ethnic identity. This Appendix concludes with summaries in French of the histories of St. Sylvester, St. Gilles, and St. Patrice.

Excerpts from the *1832 Emigrants Handbook for Arrivals in Quebec* by A.C. Buchanan (Chief of the Quebec Emigration Department) and others.

> Passengers are entitled by law to remain on board ship 48 hours after arrival; and it is unlawful for the Captain to deprive Passengers of any of their usual accommodations. Make arrangements for your journey, prior to embarkation . . . Medicine and medical advice are available at the Quebec Charitable Emigrant Society.
>
> It is particularly recommended that Emigrants not loiter at the port of landing; but to proceed to obtain settlement or employment . . . Emigrants with large families had better proceed without delay to Upper Canada (later, Ontario) or to Lower Canada (later, Quebec) . . . and if they have sons and daughters grown up, they will find demand for their service. Great caution is necessary in all your transactions. When you need advice, apply to the Government Agents (locations listed) or other respectable sources. You will be offered many plans . . . but turn away unless you are well satisfied
>
> Emigrants with families and at least 20 pounds should push immediately into the woods, in the vicinity of old settlements, where they can obtain provisions for your labor. (The difficulties, although great at first, soon subside) . . . Select a favorable spot for your log house near a spring of water or running stream and where a cellar to keep your potatoes in winter can be dug under the house . . . proceed cautiously in laying out money, but a crop of potatoes and fodder for a cow, is the first object and . . . can be accomplished the first year, if you arrive early. The second year you will be able to feed your family and the third year may find you possessing a yoke or oxen, a cow or two, a year-old calf, a couple of pigs, poultry, etc.
>
> In the Canadas, you live under British laws and constitution, and are less encumbered with taxes and local imposts than in any other country . . . The *seigniory* of St. Giles is favorably situated for Emigrants from its contiguity to the Capital and is increasing rapidly, its population is principally Irish. The Government will incur the expense of building a small log house for the temporary accommodation of settlers at their respective locations and will afford some assistance towards opening roads to the lands proposed to be settled, but will make no advances in provisions or utensils, and the settlers must depend entirely upon their own resources for bringing their lands into cultivation. (A.C. Buchanan, ***1832 Emigrants Handbook for Arrivals in Quebec***).

Irish Canadian Catholicism

Irish families emigrated during the 19th century for many reasons, including to escape long-standing conflict between Catholics and Protestants in Ireland.[52] But, the presence of Orangemen and Ribbonmen in Lotbinière County (see page 60 below) showed that some immigrants continued sectarian activism in Quebec, but without the violence. When our Catholic McKelveys emigrated from County Donegal, Irish Protestant immigrants outnumbered Irish Catholic immigrants in Canada by two to one because many Protestant Ulster Scots had previously immigrated to escape sectarian violence. Irish Protestants preferred Upper Canada (Ontario) to Lower Canada (Quebec) because, following the defeat of France in the British-French War of 1756-1763, the British allowed Quebec to retain its French culture, language, and Catholic religion.

After having been persecuted for centuries under British rule, Irish Catholics arrived in Canada with few advantages other than a familiarity with the English language and British institutions. However, the Catholic Irish brought with them a strong connection with the Roman Catholic Church—a faith they shared with French Canadians.

Canada's Catholic Church was very conservative and brought all aspects of life—secular and religious—under the control or influence of the Church. This included the creation of lay voluntary societies based in each parish under the leadership of the local priest. The Catholic Church in Canada was overwhelmingly French Canadian, so when significant numbers of Irish Catholics settled in Canada, the Church recruited priests, mostly from Ireland, who spoke English and Irish. Consequently, the Church provided the Catholic Irish with a strong institutional and community base in which to ease their integration into Canadian society.

But the presence of a growing English-speaking faithful challenged the French-speaking members of the Catholic Church, particularly in Quebec. The Church identified the retention of French as a part of their mission to preserve the social and religious order. While the Church was willing to provide Irish priests, they were not willing to provide separate services or parishes. Eventually, as French Catholics outnumbered Irish Catholics, most churches were led by French-Canadian Catholic priests and the Irish were expected to adapt. Eventually, most Irish Canadian families emigrated to the U.S.

---

[52] Over several centuries, tension continued, and violence erupted periodically in Ireland between the majority of Catholic tenant farmers and the minority of land-owning Protestants, who received land that had been seized from native Irish Catholics in the 17th century, primarily in Ulster. In 1921, when political and religious disagreements could not be resolved, Ireland was partitioned into Northern Ireland (six counties in Ulster that became part of Britain) and the Republic of Ireland, encompassing the rest of the Island. Tension and violence continued until the Good Friday Agreement of 1998 finally ended the Troubles and brought peace to Ulster.

Excerpts from "Beaurivage: Development of an Irish Ethnic Identity in Rural Quebec: 1820-1860"

D. Aidan McQuillan[53] (1942-2015) examined why few Irish Catholics assimilated into French Canadian families. His essay (https://gail25.tripod.com/que4.htm) is relevent because he studied Beaurivage,[54] during the time our ancestors lived there. His work helps explain why our McKelveys left Quebec after living there for more than forty years.

> Most Irish immigrants in the 1820s and 1830s were tenant farmers who had operated small farms in Ireland. They were ambitious, anxious to escape the constraints of tenant farming, and sought improved conditions for their children. They settled in pioneer communities on the fringes of the St. Lawrence Valley.
>
> Residents of Quebec at the time were French-speaking Roman Catholic, and rural, living on *seigneurial* (feudal French) lands along the lower St. Lawrence River. Sixty years earlier, when French colonial officials withdrew following the British conquest, a leadership vacuum developed. French clergy in the Roman Catholic Church filled the vacuum as custodians of the French Catholic national ideal.
>
> Among all immigrant groups to Quebec, Irish Catholics were the most assimilable into French Catholic society. They shared religion, were farmers and loggers, and were directed by the clergy. Their rural economies were similar and their agricultural technologies were poor. But, instead of aligning, deep rifts developed between the Irish-Catholic and Franch-Catholic communities. In the process, the Irish developed an ethnic identity and a sharpened sense of community.
>
> In 1828, a new parish of St. Sylvester was created and a church was built. In 1836, Irish-born Father Nelligan became the parish priest and served until 1851. There were occasional flare-ups, usually between Irish Catholics and Protestants. But Father Nelligan diplomatically protected the sensitivities of the Francophone and Irish Protestant minorities. *(See his photo on page 23 of this Family History).*
>
> Irish Catholics outnumbered the French by two to one, but the latter resented Irish control of the local Church board. In turn, the Irish resented French-Canadian objections to local decisions and their habit of appealing to the French church hierarchy. After Father Nelligan was re-assigned, tensions between Irish Catholics and Protestants intensified, strenthening Irish Catholic solidarity. Soon, French Canadian priests were appointed to run St. Sylvester, Irish immigration to the U.S intensified, and French Catholics eventually dominated all of Lotbinière.

---

[53] McQuillan was born in Northern Ireland, directed the Canadian Studies Program at the University of Toronto, and published dozens of books and articles on Canadian immigration, including by the Irish.

[54] Beaurivage, a large area in Lotbinière, includes the three areas where our direct McKelvey ancestors lived: St. Gilles de Beaurivage, St. Patrice de Beaurivage, and St. Sylvester de Lotbinière.

Tension between some Irish Catholics and Protestants continued after they emigrated. Ribbonmen (Irish Catholics) argued for the independence of Ireland from the U.K. while Orangemen (Irish Protestants) argued for the Protestant Ascendancy (i.e. continuation under British rule). This photo was taken near St. Sylvester on 12 July, Orangeman Day, which they celebrate with music.

Band Playing in Orangeman Day Parade, between 1890 and 1905

Photo from a video on the Facebook site of Coirneal Cealteach.

Watercolor of the St. Lawrence River in Rural Quebec, 1800s

The second part of this Appendix displays one-page histories (in French) of St. Sylvester, St. Patrice, and St. Gilles villages, developed by the Agente de Developpement Culturel de la Municipal Regional County de Lotbinière. Note the historic photos of each village.

HISTORIQUE DES MUNICIPALITÉS DE LA MRC DE LOTBINIÈRE

Marie-France St-Laurent, ethnologue
Agente de développement culturel de la MRC de Lotbinière
Projet des relais touristiques de l'Office de tourisme de Lotbinière

Saint-Sylvestre

En passant par le rang Beaurivage

Parmi toutes les municipalités de la MRC de Lotbinière, Saint-Sylvestre est celle qui est située le plus au sud. La paroisse a ainsi été nommée en 1828 en référence au nom du dernier saint du calendrier et à sa localisation à l'extrémité sud de Lotbinière et du territoire de l'archevêché de Québec.

Une partie du village vers 1910
Photo : Archives nationales du Québec

Favorisée par la construction du chemin Craig, la colonisation s'est effectuée à vive allure à compter de 1820. Dès la première moitié du 19e siècle, le territoire de la paroisse de Saint-Sylvestre a vu se bâtir un chemin, une route, 15 rangs et une concession. Ces 18 voies de colonisation ont été ouvertes sur une période de 16 ans, de 1819 à 1835, en trois étapes successives.

La colonisation du « Rang Beaurivage - Sainte-Marie-Ouest » a débuté en 1821, deux années après le début de la colonisation du chemin de Craig. Au fil des ans, ce rang est devenu la principale artère de Saint-Sylvestre puisqu'il est aussi la principale rue du village. C'est le rang le plus peuplé actuellement, en incluant le tronçon routier qui traverse le village (rue Principale). La colonisation du territoire s'est effectuée à vive allure, dès 1840, principalement par des immigrants irlandais, catholiques et protestants, fuyant la famine de leur Irlande natale.

L'érection de la paroisse catholique remonte à 1828 et la première église à 1862. À ce moment, il existait déjà une communauté irlandaise bien implantée. La toute première municipalité a été érigée en 1845, puis en 1855. Le territoire fut découpé à deux reprises, en 1871 et 1873, pour donner naissance à Saint-Patrice-de-Beaurivage et Saint-Sévérin. Les protestants implantèrent deux temples presbytériens (East et West St. Sylvester), un méthodiste (Parkhurst) et deux anglicans (St. John et St. George).

Vers 1910
Photo : Archives nationales du Québec

Rue principale vers 1910
Photo : Archives nationales du Québec

Rang Sainte-Marie ouest vers 1910
Photo : Archives nationales du Québec

Ce projet a été rendu possible grâce à la contribution de la municipalité et de ses partenaires.

Pacte rural 2007-2014
Entente de développement culturel
MRC Lotbinière
Québec

Marie-France St-Laurent, ethnologue
Agente de développement culturel de la MRC de Lotbinière
Projet des relais touristiques de l'Office de tourisme de Lotbinière

Saint-Gilles

Saint-Gilles doit son nom à Gilles Rageot qui reçut du marquis de Beauharmois et de Gilles Hocquart, gouverneur de la Nouvelle-France, la seigneurie de Beaurivage en 1738. De ce territoire se sont détachées quatre paroisses : Saint-Patrice-de-Beaurivage, Sainte-Agathe-de-Lotbinière, Saint-Narcisse-de-Beaurivage et Saint-Agapit, réduisant ainsi la population gilloise.

En 1810, le chemin Craig permit le service de diligences entre Québec et Boston. Il traversait Saint-Gilles dans toute sa longueur.

L'érection canonique de la paroisse eut lieu le 17 décembre 1828. Le premier curé, l'abbé Antoine Lebel, s'établit à Saint-Gilles en 1843. Une première église fut bâtie pour desservir la paroisse jusqu'à la construction de la nouvelle en 1882. En 1854, l'abbé Étienne Chartier, curé à Saint-Gilles, décède et, à sa demande, il fut inhumé sous le chœur de l'église d'alors et transféré sous la nouvelle église lors de sa construction. C'est en l'honneur de ce curé, défenseur des patriotes, avocat et professeur, que l'école primaire a été nommée : « École Étienne Chartier ». En 2007, à la demande de sa famille, ses restes ont été déposés dans le cimetière paroissial.

La municipalité a reçu ses lettres de noblesse en 1855

En 1876, devant l'incapacité financière des paroissiens d'entretenir un prêtre, un décret de Mgr Elzéar-Alexandre Taschereau anéantissait la paroisse. Le 14 octobre de la même année, à la suite d'un don généreux de la famille Dionne garantissant l'entretien d'un curé, une ordonnance du même évêque annulait le décret et redonnait vie à la paroisse. En 1882, on construisit l'église actuelle et, en 1914, le presbytère.

Peuplée à ses débuts de gens d'origine française, allemande, irlandaise et anglaise, Saint-Gilles a maintenant une population essentiellement francophone. Les armoiries rappellent ces pionniers et le drapeau confirme l'attachement des Gillois et Gilloises à leur territoire.

Son patrimoine bâti

En traversant Saint-Gilles, prenez le temps d'apprécier la présence de bardeaux de cèdre sur certaines maisons anciennes du village, d'admirer le souci des Gillois de conserver l'aspect architectural des maisons et bâtiments, comme l'ancien magasin général en face de l'église, fort bien conservé et bien restauré, et actuellement occupé par le petit-fils de son bâtisseur.

En entrant dans le village, direction sud à votre gauche, sur la ferme des Tailleur, on peut admirer le silo à grain, exclusivement bâti en madriers de pin. Seule construction du genre dans le territoire de la MRC.

Avec sa tourelle, le presbytère demeure un trésor d'architecture. Il est occupé en partie par la municipalité. Les élus ont à cœur la conservation de son architecture. L'église construite en 1882 renferme des trésors et les cloches activées par des cordes font également la fierté des paroissiens et paroissiennes (visite guidée possible en s'adressant au presbytère).

En continuant vers l'ouest, une maison fort bien conservée par les anciens propriétaires, entourée de vieux bâtiments de ferme, a servi tour à tour de relais de diligence, chapelle et maison familiale. Des pins centenaires l'entourent et une vigne monte le long de sa galerie (au 1761, rue Principale).

Plus loin, sur la droite (au 1916, rue Principale), trône une maison ancestrale toujours occupée par un descendant de la famille Côté. Construite par Me Alexis Côté, notaire et greffier, elle abritait la Cour des commissaires qui rendait des jugements relatifs aux causes et réclamations des habitants de Saint-Gilles.

Pour traverser la rivière Beaurivage, sur la rue Demers (route 218) vers Saint-Lambert, l'actuel pont Béland a remplacé l'ancien pont de fer Francoeur. Il doit son nom à M. Alfred Béland, propriétaire d'un moulin à bois qui, à la suite d'un incendie, a cédé sa place aux immeubles de la compagnie Élite.

Un peu plus loin dans la même direction, on découvre la rue des Industries et la rue des PME, ainsi que quelques exploitations agricoles de grande qualité.

Magasin général Demers vers 1920

Photo : Patrimoine et Histoire des seigneuries de Lotbinière

Rue Principale vers 1885
Photo : Patrimoine et Histoire des seigneuries de Lotbinière

Ce projet a été rendu possible grâce à la contribution de la municipalité et de ses partenaires.

Pacte rural 2007-2014

Entente de développement culturel

MRC Lotbinière

Québec

Marie-France St-Laurent, ethnologue
Agente de développement culturel de la MRC de Lotbinière
Projet des relais touristiques de l'Office de tourisme de Lotbinière

Saint-Patrice-de-Beaurivage

DES RACINES IRLANDAISES DANS LA SEIGNEURIE DE BEAURIVAGE

À l'origine, la municipalité de Saint-Patrice-de-Beaurivage a été implantée dans la seigneurie de Saint-Gilles concédée à Gilles Rageot de Beaurivage en 1738. Celle-ci sera vendue par la suite à Alexandre Fraser en 1782, puis à Arthur R. Ross au milieu du 19e siècle.

La colonisation de la seigneurie, dite de Beaurivage, ne prendra son envol qu'après la construction, au début des années 1800, du chemin de Craig. L'ouverture de cette voie de communication va permettre l'arrivée de 200 familles d'origine irlandaise sur le territoire de Saint-Patrice-de-Beaurivage. La population passe ainsi de 283 à 1 000 âmes en l'espace d'à peine 20 ans.

À la même époque, le seigneur Arthur Ross fait construire à Saint-Patrice-de-Beaurivage un manoir. Il apporte également des améliorations au moulin qui occupait le même emplacement que l'actuel moulin situé au coeur du village. Saint-Patrice-de-Beaurivage est maintenant prête à voler de ses propres ailes.

Toutefois, pour obtenir leur propre paroisse religieuse, ses habitants devront vivre une incroyable épopée échelonnée sur deux décennies. Essuyant refus sur refus, risquant même l'excommunion ils livreront une lutte acharnée avant de voir leur paroisse érigée canoniquement le 2 octobre 1871.

La reconnaissance civile suivra peu après, soit le 6 juin 1872. La première séance du conseil se tiendra le 11 février 1873 sous la présidence de M. Arthur Davidson Ross, maire. Les premiers procès-verbaux seront rédigés en anglais. Au début des années 1900, les citoyens de la paroisse et du village s'affrontent sur le dossier de la construction des trottoirs. Pour régler le problème, les gens du village demandent la création d'une municipalité distincte. Le 14 septembre 1921, Saint-Patrice-de-Beaurivage est séparée en deux municipalités : village et paroisse. La première séance de conseil du village sera présidée par M. Alfred Bisson, maire, le 31 octobre 1921. Il faudra patienter un peu plus de 60 ans pour qu'un décret gouvernemental sanctionne la fusion des deux municipalités en 1984.

Nouveau pont et moulin à scie vers 1928
Photo : Archives nationales du Québec

Exposition agricole à Parkhurst en 1943
Photo : Archives nationales du Québec

Photo : Patrimoine et histoire des seigneuries de Lotbinière

Ce projet a été rendu possible grâce à la contribution de la municipalité et de ses partenaires.

Pacte rural 2007-2014

Entente de développement culturel

MRC Lotbinière

Culture, Communications et Condition féminine Québec

Appendix Six

John and Lawrence McKelvey's Canadian Farm and their Records

The McKelvey's Canadian Farm

Steve Cameron located the 1851 Agricultural Census for Lawrence McKelvey's farm, and he visited the former site of the farm on St. John's Range, took photos, and spoke with the current owner of the land. According to the Agricultural Census, Lawrence had 2 acres of potatoes, 4 milk cows, 2 calves, 2 horses and 4 sheep. Steve remarked that the McKelveys had good access to food within 20 years of settlement, and not all Irish immigrants had horses at the time. The current owner is a French-Canadian, like nearly all residents of Quebec at this time. The owner told Steve that he owns 4 lots including the old McKelvey farm. His home is on an adjoining lot because there was no house on the McKelvey's former farm when he purchased it.

McKelvey's former 800 acre farm on St. John's Range, April 2023

The edge of their former farm is shown in the foreground in the photo on the left.
The farm is narrow and long, extending to a road on the far right (not shown). See map on page 20.

Photos taken by Steve Cameron who noted that the McKelvey's former farm is on a hill, with a view (in the distance) of the hills on the north side of the St. Lawrence River towards Quebec City.

Typical late 19th-century rural Quebec farm

Source: Clarence Gagnon, Quebec-born post-impressionist painter, 1881-1942

John and Lawrence McKelvey's Canadian Records

The following eight pages display four documents from the Quebec Archives, provided by Steve Cameron (thank you for your help!).

1. Pages 66-67: Land rental agreement, 05 October 1839, between John McKelvey and a local land-owning *seigneur* (see footnote 30). These agreements allowed tenants to purchase the land they farmed with "rent" payments over time, typically 10 years. This agreement covered land on St. John's Range and on St. Patricks' Range, in what is now the village. The notary was Daniel Bryne, a popular Irish-Catholic notary in St. Sylvester from 1837 to the 1880s.

2. Pages 68-72: John McKelvey's Last Will and Testament, 05 April 1860, five pages (with summary), before notary Daniel Bryne.

3. Page 73: Deed of sale, 03 May 1881, one page. John's son Lawrence sold the McKelvey family farm (with buildings) on St. John's Range to William Moran before notary C. O. Gagne, for $1200, a substantial amount at the time.

4. Page 73: Immigration/naturalization form, 07 November 1881, indicating that Lawrence entered the United States at Port Huron, Michigan in July 1881.

Locomotive from the Grand Trunk Railway, c. 1859

In 1881, Lawrence likely travelled on the Grand Trunk Railway from Craig's Road Station (near St. Sylvester) via Montreal and Toronto to Sarnia in Ontario, Canada. Sarnia is directly across the St. Clair River from Port Huron, Michigan.

Page 1 of 05 October 1839 Land Rent Agreement for John McKelvey

No. 375. 5 Octr. 1839. Oblig. 386

Jno. McKelvey to Seig. St. Giles

BEFORE the undersigned Notaries Publics for the Province of Lower Canada, residing at in the District of Quebec.

PERSONALLY APPEARED John McKelvey of St. Sylvester, Farmer

Who has acknowledged and confessed himself to be indebted to Jane Davidson, Widow of the late David Ross, in his lifetime of the City of Montreal, in the District of Montreal, and Province aforesaid, Advocate, Seignioress in possession of one undivided half of the Fief and Seigniory of St. Giles dit Beaurivage in the County of Lotbinière and District of Quebec, and to Alexander Mackay of the said City, Physician, Seignior in possession of one undivided fourth part of the said Fief and Seigniory, and to Robert Mackay of the said City, Advocate, Seignior in possession of one undivided fourth part of the said Fief and Seigniory, (the said Seigniors and Seignioress appearing and accepting this recognizance, by their Attorney, Gustavus William Wicksteed, of the City of Quebec, in the County and District of Quebec, Advocate,) in the sum of four pounds eight shillings and six pence Currency: that is to say,

1st Cap. del. to Seigrs. 13/2/40

for for arrears of Cens et Rentes to the first day of March last, on number four in the concession of St Patrick's, bounded in front by the River Beaurivage, in the rear by the end of the concession, to the north east by number five and to the South west by number three and containing ninety superficial arpents more or less — and on lot number six in the concession of St. John's bounded in front and rear by the roads [illegible] of the concession to the South East by number seven and to the north west by number five, and containing ninety superficial arpents more or less —

of which said lands he the said John McKelvey

acknowledges and avows himself to be in possession as Proprietor, and to hold the same *en roture* in the *censive* and *mouvance* of the Fief and Seigniory aforesaid, under and by virtue of the conditions, clauses, terms, conditions and provisos of the original Deeds of Concession of the said land respectively, whereby the said lands are subject to the annual payment to the Domain of the said Seigniory of the *Cens et Rentes* hereinafter mentioned; that is to say:—

one pound Currency — for each of the said lots making two pounds Currency for both —

Continuation of Page 1 of 05 October 1839 Land Rent Agreement for John McKelvey

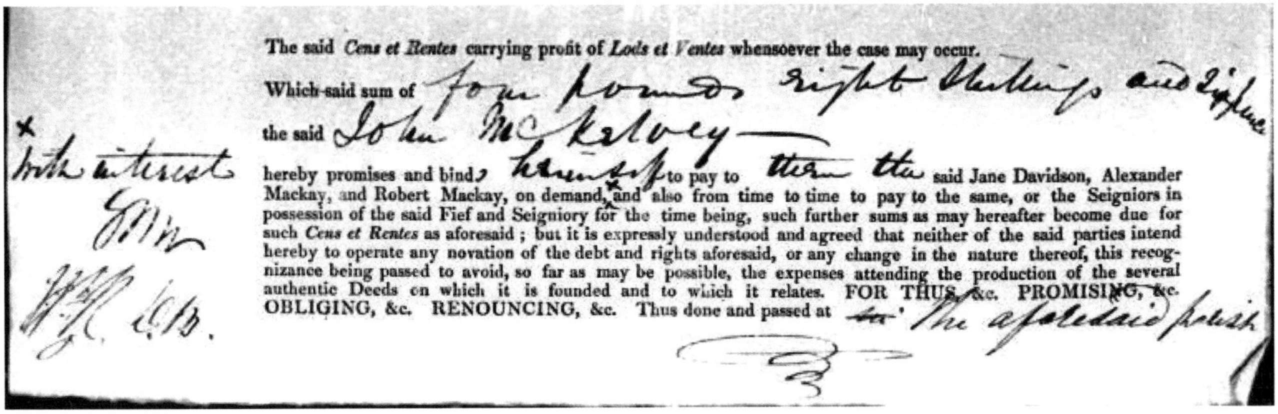

The said *Cens et Rentes* carrying profit of *Lods et Ventes* whensoever the case may occur.

Which said sum of four pounds eight shillings and six pence

the said John McKelvey

hereby promises and binds himself to pay to them the said Jane Davidson, Alexander Mackay, and Robert Mackay, on demand, x and also from time to time to pay to the same, or the Seigniors in possession of the said Fief and Seigniory for the time being, such further sums as may hereafter become due for such *Cens et Rentes* as aforesaid; but it is expressly understood and agreed that neither of the said parties intend hereby to operate any novation of the debt and rights aforesaid, or any change in the nature thereof, this recognizance being passed to avoid, so far as may be possible, the expenses attending the production of the several authentic Deeds on which it is founded and to which it relates. FOR THUS, &c. PROMISING, &c. OBLIGING, &c. RENOUNCING, &c. Thus done and passed at the aforesaid parish

x with interest

Page Two of 05 October 1839 Land Rent Agreement for John McKelvey

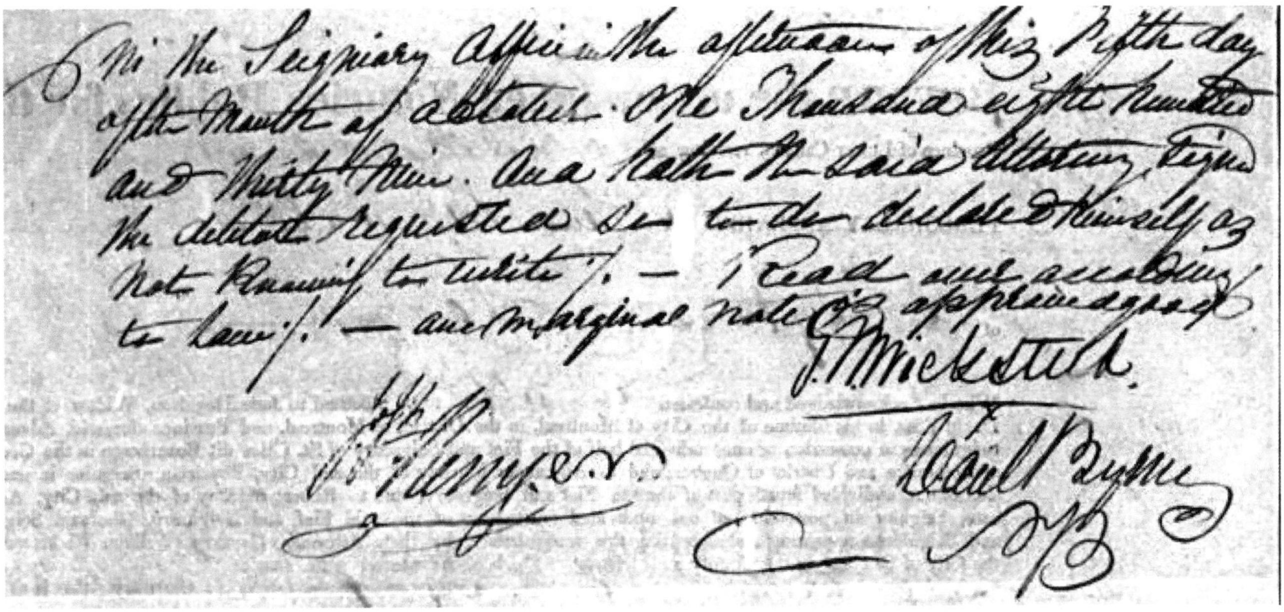

in the Seigniory office in the afternoon of this fifth day of the Month of October One Thousand eight hundred and thirty nine. And hath the said obligor requested so to declare himself as not knowing to write /. — Read and according to law /. — one marginal note approved good

Last Will and Testament of John McKelvey (1771-1860)

The four-page Will is reproduced on the following pages, but it is hard to read. Steven Cameron generously extracted information from this document, noting the following key points. According to Steve, the will clearly:

1. is dated 05 April, 1860 and was prepared by Daniel Byrne, the "notary of choice" among the Irish in St. Sylvester. Byrne refers to McKelvey as a yeoman, a common term for farmer;

2. was taken with "certainty" of death approaching but McKelvey was in good mental state;

3. confirms McKelvey's wishes as a Roman Catholic including requesting forgiveness;

4. asks for all debts to be paid;

5. leaves almost everything to his "beloved son Lawrence," including: (1) a lot of 50 acres (English measure) in Wolfestown that is part of lot 26 on the 8th range, likely without buildings; and (2) a lot of 90 arpents (French measure) in St. Sylvester (eventually St. Patrick) that is lot 6 of St. John range;

6. is witnessed by son-in-law James Plunkett and nephew Patrick Gormle. They sign the will with their names; and

7. is "signed" by John with an X.

Steven notes that he cannot decipher other parts of the Will. John seems to:

1. exclude his children other than Lawrence, although the will was witnessed by James Plunkett [the spouse of John's daughter Mary (McKelvey) Plunkett] and Patrick Gormley [the son of John's daughter Susan (McKelvey) Gormley].

2. suggest (but not require) that Lawrence provide his siblings with payments of (cannot read the number) English shillings; and

3. not mention other property, such as cattle, horses, carriages, or house furnishings.

2150
No. ~~1911~~. } 5 April, 1860 } Last will of
Jno. McKelvey }

1st copy del to Legatee 10/4/61 (W.S.)
2nd copy del. to the Legatee 24/10/72 (W.S.)

On this fifth day of April in
the year of our Lord one thousand
and eight hundred and sixty
at four of the clock in the afternoon, before us the subscribing
Notary Public, duly commissioned
and sworn in and for the province
of Lower Canada residing in the
parish of St. Sylvester in the district
of Quebec, and the witnesses hereinafter mentioned and also subscribing, personally came and appeared
and was present John McKelvey
of the parish of St. Sylvester in
the aforesaid district of Quebec,
yeoman, of sound and dispo-
sing mind memory judgment
and understanding thus as he
appeared unto the said Notary
and witnesses by his words and
actions, who considering the certainty of death and the uncertain-
ty of the hour and approach
did request us to draw up his
last will and testament in
the form and manner fol-
lowing, that is to say:—
1°. As a Roman Catholic and
apostolic Christian the said
testator recommends his soul
to Almighty God, supplicating
his divine Majesty through the
infinite merits of Jesus Christ
to pardon him his offences
and

Forever and him eternal bea-
titude
2°. Wills the said testator by this
his last will and testament that
all his just debts be paid by his
testamentary executor to take on
the ... for this instrument ...
3°. Wills and bequeaths the
said testator by this his last
will and testament to his dearly
beloved son Lawrence McKelvey
of said St. Sylvester yeoman
only all and every the property ~~...~~
~~moveable and immoveable~~ im-
J. L. — moveable + that he shall or
may die possessed of to
D. B. be by him used and disposed
of for posterity as he shall or
may think proper and more
especially the quantity of fifty superficial acres of land English
Measure being the ~~North~~ East quarter
\+ of lot of land Number twenty in
South West the Eighth Range of the Township
L. D. of Wolfstown, in the District of
~~...~~, being a free Grant
D. B. to the said testator from the
Provincial Government
~~...~~ the said testator
declaring that he ceded and
made over gratuitously to
his said well beloved son
Lawrence McKelvey the whole
of lot of land number six in
the Concession St. John in the
~~of~~ said parish of St. Sylvester
of ninety superficial arpens
more

Page 3 of 05 April 1860 Last Will and Testament of John McKelvey (1771-1860)

[illegible] with all the buildings
thereon erected without any
reserve whatsoever by deed
of cession passed before Mr.
John Walsh and his colleague
the twenty ninth day of April
one thousand eight hundred
and forty one, without thereby in
them allowing any sum of money
as consideration to his other
children issue of his marriage
with his late deceased wife
Mary Sleevin, then the said
testator desires that his said
son Lawrence shall not be
troubled, molested nor in
any wise disturbed in the [illegible]
session and enjoyment of the
the said lot of land [illegible]
by his brothers Edward and sisters
by this his last will and testament
ratifying and confirming the said
recited deed of cession [illegible]
wills and bequeaths to his said
well beloved son Lawrence
the said lot of land [illegible],
[illegible] in said St. John's concession, St. Sylvester, appurte-
nances and dependencies thereof
without any reserve whatsoever
of the said testator by this his last
will and testament instituting
the said Lawrence McKelvey for
his general and universal legatee
of all the said property at the
charge by the the said legatee
to pay to [illegible] said [illegible]
each the sum of one English shilling
to [illegible] [illegible]
stead of all rights [illegible]
[illegible]

6 [illegible] and immediately pa-
ternal and Maternal that they
might or could in future pretend
to have in the further Estate of
the said testator, revoking the
said testator by this his last
will and testament all other
wills testaments and Codicils
which he may have previously
made notwithstanding his [illegible]
with any thereof save these presents, the which he declares to
only Contain his real intention
and last will.
And to execute the said last will
and testament the said testator doth name and appoint
his said dearly beloved Lawrence
who has [illegible] him-
self of all the said property
according to the Rules, customs laws and usages of
Lower Canada. Thus done
and dictated named and made
by the said testator to us the said
said Notaries in presence of
James Plunket and Patrick Gorraly
both yeoman of said St Sylvester
[illegible] witnesses expressly
called in and after that the
presents were made and read
by us the said Notaries, the witnesses
present in said and declared that
he understood them well declaring
them to contain his real intention
and last will and having persisted
[illegible] not knowing to sign made his
mark as a cross with us the said
Notaries the witnesses. Three marginal
notes signed good. Five words erased null.

at the actual domicile of the said Lawrence McKelvey in the Number Nineteen [illegible] and further

J. P.
P. G.
[illegible]

James Plunket

Patrick Gormley

John his X mark McKelvey

Dan'l Byrne N.P.

03 May 1881 Deed of Sale Transferring the McKelvey Family Farm on St. John's Range from Lawrence McKelvey to William Moran for $1,200, a substantial amount at that time.

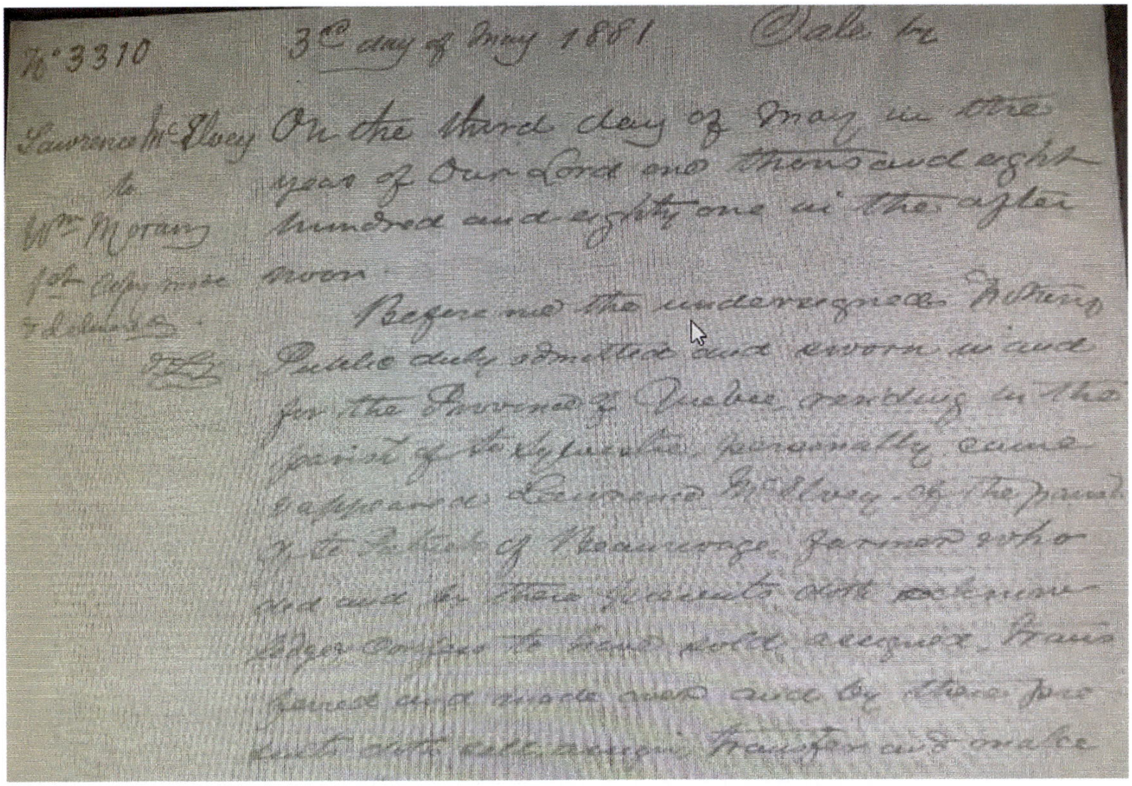

N° 3310 3rd day of May 1881 Sale by

Lawrence McElvey to Wm Moran

1st Copy made & delivered

On the third day of May in the year of Our Lord one thousand eight hundred and eighty one in the after noon.

Before me the undersigned Notary Public duly admitted and sworn in and for the Province of Quebec residing in the parish of St Sylvestre personally came & appeared Lawrence McElvey of the parish of St Patrick of Beaurivage farmer who did and by these presents doth acknow ledge confess to have sold, acquit, trans ferred and made over and by these pre sents doth sell assign transfer and make

07 November 1881 Naturalization document of Lawrence McKelvey who entered the U.S. on July 1881 at Port Huron, Michigan.

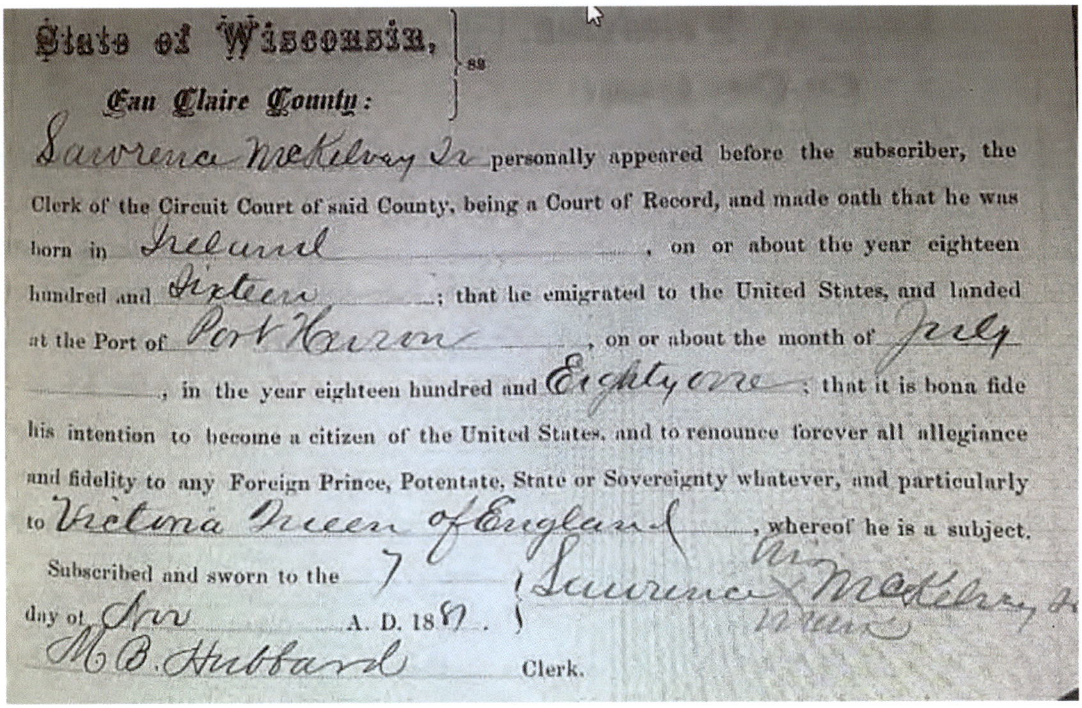

State of Wisconsin, } ss
Eau Claire County: }

Lawrence McKelvey Jr personally appeared before the subscriber, the Clerk of the Circuit Court of said County, being a Court of Record, and made oath that he was born in Ireland, on or about the year eighteen hundred and Sixteen; that he emigrated to the United States, and landed at the Port of Port Huron, on or about the month of July, in the year eighteen hundred and Eighty one; that it is bona fide his intention to become a citizen of the United States, and to renounce forever all allegiance and fidelity to any Foreign Prince, Potentate, State or Sovereignty whatever, and particularly to Victoria Queen of England, whereof he is a subject.

Subscribed and sworn to the 7 day of Nov A. D. 1881.

M. B. Hubbard Clerk.

Lawrence his X mark McKelvey Jr

Appendix Seven

Grandfather John M. McKelvey (1885-1935) in California

Events in the Life of John M. McKelvey

Year	Age	Event and Location	Data Source[55]
1885	0	Birth, Eau Claire, Eau Claire Co., Wisconsin	Wisconsin, Births and Christening Index, 1801-1928
1900	15	Living at 221 Tawas Street with parents and siblings in Alpena, Michigan	1900 U.S. Federal Census
1910	25	Living on Fillmore Street in San Francisco with "wife" (no marriage certificate located), daughter (our mother, Helen McKelvey) and stepson (our uncle Jimmy Conner). Worked at cigar stand.	1910 U.S. Federal Census
1915	30	Living at 1774 O'Farrell Street. Selling cigars at 1360 Fillmore Street in San Francisco.	1915 San Francisco City Directory
1918	33	Living in Truckee, California, and working as a brakeman on the Southern Pacific Railroad	U.S. WWI Draft Registration
1920	35	Living at 1920 Bridge Street in Truckee (in Meadow Lake census area) with brother Lawrence. Merchant selling cigars.	1920 U.S. Federal Census
1930	45	Living in the (Larry) McKelvey Apartment Building at 78 East High Street in Truckee, selling soft drinks at a stand. Note that Wing Wong, the cook at Larry McKelvey's saloon, also lived in the McKelvey Apartments.	1930 U.S. Federal Census
1935	50	Died suddenly on March 22 in Stockton, San Joaquin County, CA. Burial in St. Mary's Catholic Cemetery, Sacramento, Sacramento County, CA	Obituary, March 23, 1935, *Sacramento Bee*

[55] View the records on my Ancestry family tree under username joycevkelly66.

According to family lore, John took a job on a ranch in Sacramento County sometime after 1900.[56] There, he met our grandmother Josephine (Theobald) Conner. Josephine was married to William Conner who may have owned the ranch or been a ranch hand like John. William and Josephine had two children–our Uncle Jimmie and Aunt Gertie. Josephine left William for John and they lived in Truckee, where our mother, Helen June (McKelvey) Kelly was born in 1906. There is no evidence that they married, and John reported himself "single" on the U.S. Federal Census for the rest of his life.

By the 1910 U.S. Federal Census, John (age 25) and Josephine (age 30) were living in San Francisco with our mother (age 4) and our uncle Jimmie, age 11 (we don't know where Aunt Gertie was living at the time). On the 1915 San Francisco City Directory, John listed his employment as a merchant, selling cigars and soft drinks in a stand. Sometime between 1915 and 1918,[57] John left San Francisco and returned to Truckee. On the 1920 U.S. Federal Census, John reported living with his older brother Lawrence in Truckee.

Life in Truckee

Lawrence owned a small apartment building, McKelvey Apartments, at 78 East High Street in Truckee (the lot is now vacant) where John lived during the 1930 U.S. Federal Census. Lawrence also owned a number of saloons in Truckee where John worked as a bartender. In 1905, Lawrence sold the Kirk Inn Saloon and moved to CalNeva, where he lived for ten years. Returning to Truckee in 1915, Lawrence bought the Truckee Saloon. In 1916, Lawrence also owned the Truckee Billiard Hall.

Prohibition started in 1920. At that point, Lawrence bought the Capitol (formerly Hurd) Saloon. By 1923, Lawrence owned "The Truckee, Home of the Workingman" on Front Street.[58] During Prohibition, many saloons operated as speakeasies, advertising sodas and cigars while serving alcohol in the basement or other hidden room. Tahoe historian Mark McLaughlin described the prominence of saloons in the development of the West in the *Tahoe Daily Tribune* on 23 December 2015.

> . . . As the male population in the West boomed, so did the number of saloons ready to slake their thirst. By the time the transcontinental railroad came through Truckee in 1868, there were 35 residences and 28 saloons and dance halls. The saloon was all things to all men. Besides being a drinking establishment, it was often an eatery, hotel, bath and comfort station, livery stable, gambling den, dance hall, bordello, barbershop,

[56] On the 1900 U.S. Federal Census, John was 15 years old and living with his parents and siblings in Alpena, Michigan.

[57] John registered for the WWI Draft on 12 September 1918. He reported living in Truckee, CA and working as a brakeman on the Southern Pacific Railroad. He listed his mother as next of kin.

[58] Thank you to Mrs. Chaun Owens-Mortier, a volunteer researcher at the Truckee-Donner Historical Society, for finding and forwarding advertisements from local newspapers for Lawrence's saloons.

courtroom, political arena, dueling ground and undertaker's parlor. The saloon was as American as apple pie.

Meanwhile, on the Eastern Coast of the country, Benjamin Franklin tipped the bottle frequently; John Hancock was a rumrunner while George Washington drank hot toddies in countless taprooms and ran up enormous liquor bills.

Saloons in the West drew men like a magnet. For some of the early prospectors and pioneers, whiskey came before food, women – even gold. The saloon was often the first building in a new community and the last to close before it became a ghost town. The saloon was the best place for socializing and conducting business, and the barkeep was one of the most respected citizens in town.

Mark Twain wrote, "The cheapest and easiest way to become an influential man and be looked up to by the community at large was to stand behind a bar, wear a cluster-diamond pin, and sell whiskey." After visiting Virginia City, Nevada, Twain added, ". . . the saloon keeper held a higher rank than any other member of society. His opinion had weight. It was his privilege to say how elections should be run. No great movement could succeed without the countenance and direction of the saloon keeper."

In 1860, the total population of Virginia City was 2,390, only 118 of whom were women. Without the restraining influence of respectable women, miners often drank until they passed out. In many saloons, itinerant wayfarers who spent money on drink were allowed to sleep on the sawdust floor . . . (Excerpts and photo below, from the *Tahoe Daily Tribune*, 23 December 2015, by Mark McLaughlin.)

19th/20th-century Saloon in Truckee

Source: Truckee-Donner Historical Society, re-published in the *Tahoe Daily Tribune*, 23 December 2015. This photo was colorized on MyHeritage.com.

The Truckee-Donner Historical Society website, https://www.truckeehistory.org, has relevant materials including articles written by Guy Coates, a research historian and former VP of the Society. Here are excerpts from one article:

How Truckee Survived Prohibition by Guy Coates

> . . . On January 16, 1920, prohibition of the sale and consumption of alcohol became law, sanctioned under the Volstead Act. This unpopular law carried with it some heavy penalties; including fines of up to $1,000 and those unable to pay their fines faced a six-month jail term. Millions of Americans who enjoyed an occasional drink either made their own brews at home or, more often, bought their beer or whiskey from "bootleggers" who earned an illegal, sometimes dangerous, but remunerative living supplying it. "Speakeasies," illegal saloons, soon flourished across the country. Truckee was no exception. After World War I many of the local sawmills had closed and the ice industry had declined.
>
> Accustomed to hardship and traditionally rebellious, Truckee's enterprising citizens found ways to survive. Saloons became "Soda Fountains." Illegal stills popped up everywhere. It wasn't unusual to find a distillery in the basement homes of even the most respectable citizens. In a 1997 interview, the late Karl Kielhofer described one of Truckee's speakeasies, known as the "Silver Mirror," that his father, Moke, along with Dan Smith operated in the Rex Hotel building. "It had a front door with peep holes that opened electrically," Kielhofer said. "Once you got inside, you entered a cage where they could get a good look at you from two or three different angles. If you looked OK, they'd let you in. Inside, you could buy whiskey for a dollar a shot and play games."
>
> Truckee's saloon keepers would pay off officials in Nevada County and they would warn them when the raids by the "Pro-Hi's" (Federal agents) were going to come. Whenever the saloon keepers got caught, they had a volunteer who would go to jail for them. The Silver Mirror had a guy named Joe Lawrence who always went to jail for my dad. Every saloon had a person who was willing to go to jail for the owner. Larry McKelvey was running the Capitol Saloon. They called him the 'Grey Wolf.' His brother, Jack McKelvey, worked for him and he had a Chinese cook named Wing Wong.[59]
>
> Dave Cabona was Truckee's 'Czar' or 'Godfather' and he had the 'in' with the sheriff in Nevada County. Kielhofer recalled the many boarding houses on River Street, operated by Truckee's sizeable Italian population, that served the ice cutters and woodcutters. "Every boarding house was a night club," recalled Kielhofer. "My father, whose mother was Italian, made whiskey at his home on East River Street. Everyone had a basement in those days where whiskey and wine were made.
>
> Reno was run by casino owners Graham and McKay. They owned the old Bank Club, a racetrack, race horses, and were involved in many questionable schemes. In fact, both were finally sent to the federal penitentiary. Graham and McKay put out the word that Truckee was to be a safe haven. Baby Face Nelson, Alvin Karpis, Pretty Boy Floyd and Machine Gun Kelly spent time in Truckee.

---

[59] Wing Wong is listed as living in the McKelvey Apartments on the 1930 U.S. Federal Census.

Graham and McKay made it clear there was to be no trouble in Truckee and there were never any violent incidents from this crowd, although they would sometimes get drunk and pilfer from some local store or get in a fight. Graham and McKay would always arrive, or send an emissary to pay-off the merchant so he wouldn't file charges. Occasionally, some of the lesser-known gang members came to Truckee with their families and stayed for a while. One worked for Larry McKelvey at the Capitol, dealing cards. He was reputed to have been with the Capone gang in Chicago.

The town was generally calm during the week, but on weekends when the lumberjacks, ice-cutters, section hands from the railroad and the crews from Floriston arrived, it was a rough and tumble situation. The fights that broke out sometimes got out of control. Bodies would sometimes be found dumped at the cemetery after these weekends. Another problem arose when 'toughs' riding the rails would mistakenly believe that Truckee was easy picking and stir things up only to learn that Truckee businesses were able to take care of themselves. The so-called 'toughs' always ended up leaving on the next freight.

Local enforcement of the Volstead Act was spotty across the nation, and most police were more than happy to leave it up to the Federal Agents or the Pro-Hi's as they were nicknamed. In Truckee, the pay for the police, at least my dad's pay, came from local merchants, many of whom were bootleggers themselves; so police said, let the 'Feds' do it, although he was called in several times to help the sheriff with his 'raids.' Dave Cabona always knew when these raids were coming so arrests were few."

In a 1997 interview, the late Gene Barton disclosed some interesting revelations: "Truckee was the biggest bootlegging area on the west coast," said Barton. "Whenever the Pro-Hi's came to town they'd go into a saloon, order a shot of whiskey, then arrest the bartender and close the saloon for thirty days. After the bartender got out of jail, they'd be back in business again. Everyone drank in those days, and nobody considered it wrong. All a bootlegger needed to make was $25 per day to stay in business. All business establishments had basements where whisky and wine were stored." "Whiskey made in Truckee was considered some of the best on the North American continent," said Barton. "It was made from sugar, wheat and barley and aged in old wooden barrels and they strained it well, so it wasn't bad for you."

The constable at the time, Butch Boettcher, knew about all the bootlegging but didn't enforce the laws. I believe he got his share of the action. If someone needed to hide, he and other locals would help. Boettcher never put anyone in jail. Tony Polyanich's club had the best whiskey. The Capitol was also popular. Charlie and Bertha Hope, a vaudeville couple, had the Gilt-Edge Saloon, later called the Pastime Club.

As Truckee's reputation as a hub for the sale of illegal alcohol grew, so did pressure from law enforcement agencies. On March 10, 1921, the following story appeared in the *Truckee Republican*: "Prohibition enforcement officers (pro-hi's) raided the homes of Pete Denosta, Hank Wilsie and C.F. Painter. At Denosta's home, 150 gallons of mash and 75 gallons of wine were found. At Wilsie's house officers found four stills in operation along with 15 gallons of Jackass Brandy and 350 gallons of mash. A still was found in operation at the house of C.F. Painter along with a quantity of brandy and mash. Eight gallons of Jackass Brandy were found in the home of Ed Baldwin, but no charges were filed. (Excerpted from "How Truckee Survived Prohibition," by Guy Coates, posted to https://www.truckeehistory.org).

In February 1933, Congress passed the 21st amendment that repealed prohibition. On December 5th, the 21st Amendment was ratified.

Jibboom Street, Truckee, 1870 (see page 80 of this Family History)

Downtown Truckee at the end of the 19th century

Source of photos: Truckee-Donner Historical Society images published in *Images of Truckee*, Sherry E. Jennings, Acadia Publishing, 2011. I colorized the photos on MyHeritage.com

The top map, dated June 1938, shows land with buildings owned by Larry M. McKelvey and others, between East Main Street (renamed Jibboom Street) and an alley in central Truckee. Jibbom Street housed the red light district from c. 1860-1953. The bottom map is a current Google aerial view of the same area with the alley on the bottom.

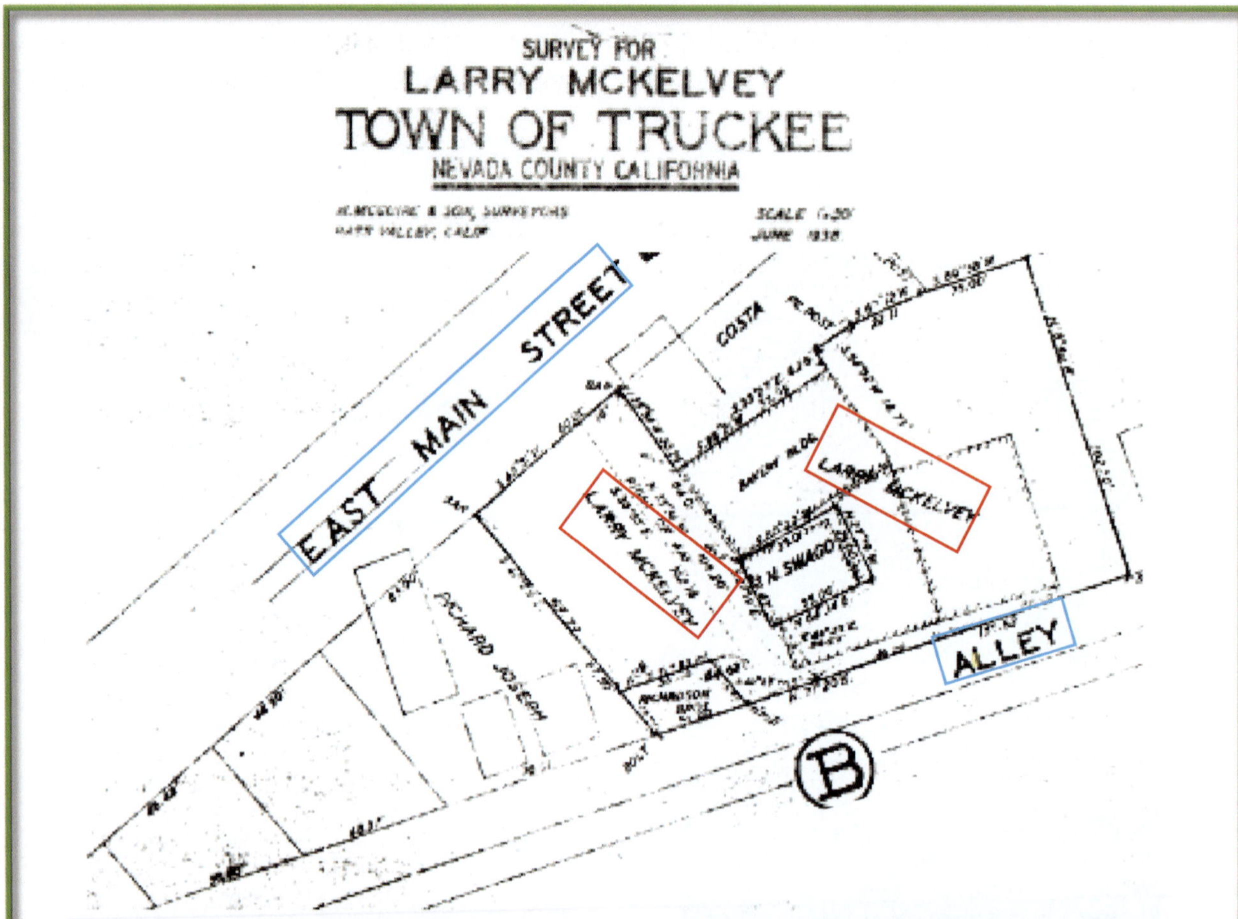

Thank you to Mrs. Chaun Owens-Mortier, a volunteer researcher at the Truckee-Donner Historical Society, for locating and providing the clippings on pages 81-82.

John M. McKelvey WWI Draft Registration Card, September 12, 1918

REGISTRATION CARD

SERIAL NUMBER 41 ORDER NUMBER 1152

1 John Michael McKelvey

2 PERMANENT HOME ADDRESS: Truckee . Calif

Age in Years 3 33 Date of Birth 4 January 12th 1885

RACE: White 5 ✓

U. S. CITIZEN: Native Born 10 ✓

PRESENT OCCUPATION 16 Brakeman

EMPLOYER'S NAME 17 Southern Pac. R.R. Co

18 PLACE OF EMPLOYMENT OR BUSINESS: Sacramento Calif

NEAREST RELATIVE Name 19 Mrs-Katherine McKelvey Address 20 Alpena Mich

I AFFIRM THAT I HAVE VERIFIED ABOVE ANSWERS AND THAT THEY ARE TRUE. John Michael McKelvey

P. M. G. O. Form No. 1 (Red)

REGISTRAR'S REPORT 4-3-11.C

DESCRIPTION OF REGISTRANT

HEIGHT: Medium ✓ BUILD: Medium ✓ COLOR OF EYES: Blue COLOR OF HAIR: Black

29 Has person lost arm, leg, hand, eye, or is he obviously physically disqualified? (Specify.) No

30 I certify that my answers are true; that the person registered has read or has had read to him his own answers; that I have witnessed his signature or mark, and that all of his answers of which I have knowledge are true, except as follows:

A. J. Mickel

Date of Registration Sept-12-1918

~~DIVISION NO.~~ 2 ~~CITY of SACRAMENTO~~ ~~CALIFORNIA~~ Local Board for the County of Nevada, State of California. Nevada City, California

(STAMP OF LOCAL BOARD)

John M. McKelvey fined $50 under national prohibition act for possession of liquor

September 12, 1927, *Sacramento Bee*, page 8

FEDERAL COURT OPENS SESSION; THREE FINED

The Fall session of the federal court convened at 10 A. M. to-day with Federal Judge A. F. St. Sure of San Francisco presiding. Assistant United States Attorney Albert E. Sheets is prosecuting all criminal cases for the government.

Three national prohibition act violators were tried and convicted at the morning session and a number of prohibition cases were continued until the afternoon court session.

James Smith of Marysville pleaded guilty to a charge of sale of intoxicating liquor and was ordered to pay a $200 fine. A plea of guilty was entered by John McKelvey of Truckee to a possession charge and a fine of $50 was imposed upon him. A $100 fine was paid by Lawrence Shoopman of Marysville when he pleaded guilty to a possession charge.

Woman killed and others injured when car driven by John McKelvey crashes

October 19, 1931, *San Bernardino Sun*

Woman Attorney Is Killed on Highway

(By Associated Press)

SACRAMENTO, Oct. 18.—Miss Hester Mayotte, 45, prominent Reno woman attorney, was killed today on the state highway one-half mile south of Colfax, when she was thrown from the rumble seat of a speeding roadster to the top of the car, then crushed as the machine turned over after careening up a steep bank. Four other persons were injured.

They are: Horace Davis, Truckee, broken back; J. R. Egan, Fresno, broken leg; Mrs. Egan, bruises and lacerations; and John McKelvey, Truckee, driver of the car, serious cuts and shock.

John was committed to Stockton State (Mental) Hospital (hospital record not displayed) on February 26, 1935—the day a jury declared him insane. See the newsclip below on the right

Jack M. and Lawrence McKelvey purchase Truckee lot, June 2, 1934, *Morning Union.*

No. 4194—Jack M. and Lawrence P. McKelvey—In Truckee Lot on S side of Main St. East com. at NW Cor. of John Grays Corral lot thence W 60 ft. along Main St. East thence SE 72½ ft. thence E 30 ft. thence S 15 ft. thence E 24.62 ft. thence N 108.20 ft. to place of beginning. In Truckee Lot commencing at 34 ft. SE of NW Cor. of Gray's Corral Lot and running 35 ft. SE thence 84 ft. E thence 35 ft. N thence 84 ft. to place of beginning with Imps. In Truckee strip of land on N side of alley in SW Cor. of John Gray Corral Lot being 46 ft. on alley from E to West and 17 ft. in width with Imps. In Truckee Lot on alley in rear of Blk B commencing 46 ft. E of SW Cor. of John Gray Corral Lot thence E 55 ft. on alley by 102 ft. deep with Imps. In Truckee E 2½ ft. of Lot 12 and W 20 ft. of Lot 13 Blk B with Imps. In Truckee all of Lot 19 and 1 foot of Lot 20 Blk B with Imps. Personal property. Total amount due $434.48.

John McKelvey found insane by jury Feb.27, 1935, *Morning Union, p. 2*

McKelvey Is Found Insane by Examining Jury

One of the few insanity trials before a jury ever held in this county was heard in the superior court in a charge of insanity against John M. McKelvey of Truckee. The defendant had been brought to the county seat from Truckee during the past week, complaint having been made that his actions seemed to indicate that he had lost his mind.

Judge Tuttle being absent in Los Angeles under assignment of the State Judicial Council, McKelvey was taken to Auburn for examination as to his mental condition. There he was informed of his right to a jury trial and he demanded that right.

The matter was set for yesterday morning before a jury selected from a special venire with Judge J. B. Landis of Auburn persiding.

When the trial was called it appeared that the defendant was without counsel and financially unable to employ an attorney and Frank B. Finnegan was appointed by the court to look after the defendant's rights. District Attorney Vernon Stoll appeared for the People.

A number of witnesses were examined and the case was submitted to the jury which returned a verdict finding the defendant to be insane after a deliberation of ten minutes. He will be taken to the state hospital today.

The following composed the jury: R. A. Paine, Charles Steffens, William Grigg, W. F. Buhl, P. A. Kelly, Dennis Coughlan, H. W. Brown, William Mutton, Clayton Chatfield, John Harris, L. Courtright and George E. Walling.

The Certificate of Death below shows that John died, at age 50, of alcoholic meningitis (he also had alcoholic psychosis) on March 22, 1936 in Stockton State (Mental) Hospital. This was less than one month after he was declared insane at a jury trial and admitted to the Hospital. Meningitis is a contagious disease to which alcoholics are especially susceptible. It was a common cause of death in group settings until the mid-20th century.

State of California Certificate of Death, John McKelvey, March 22, 1936

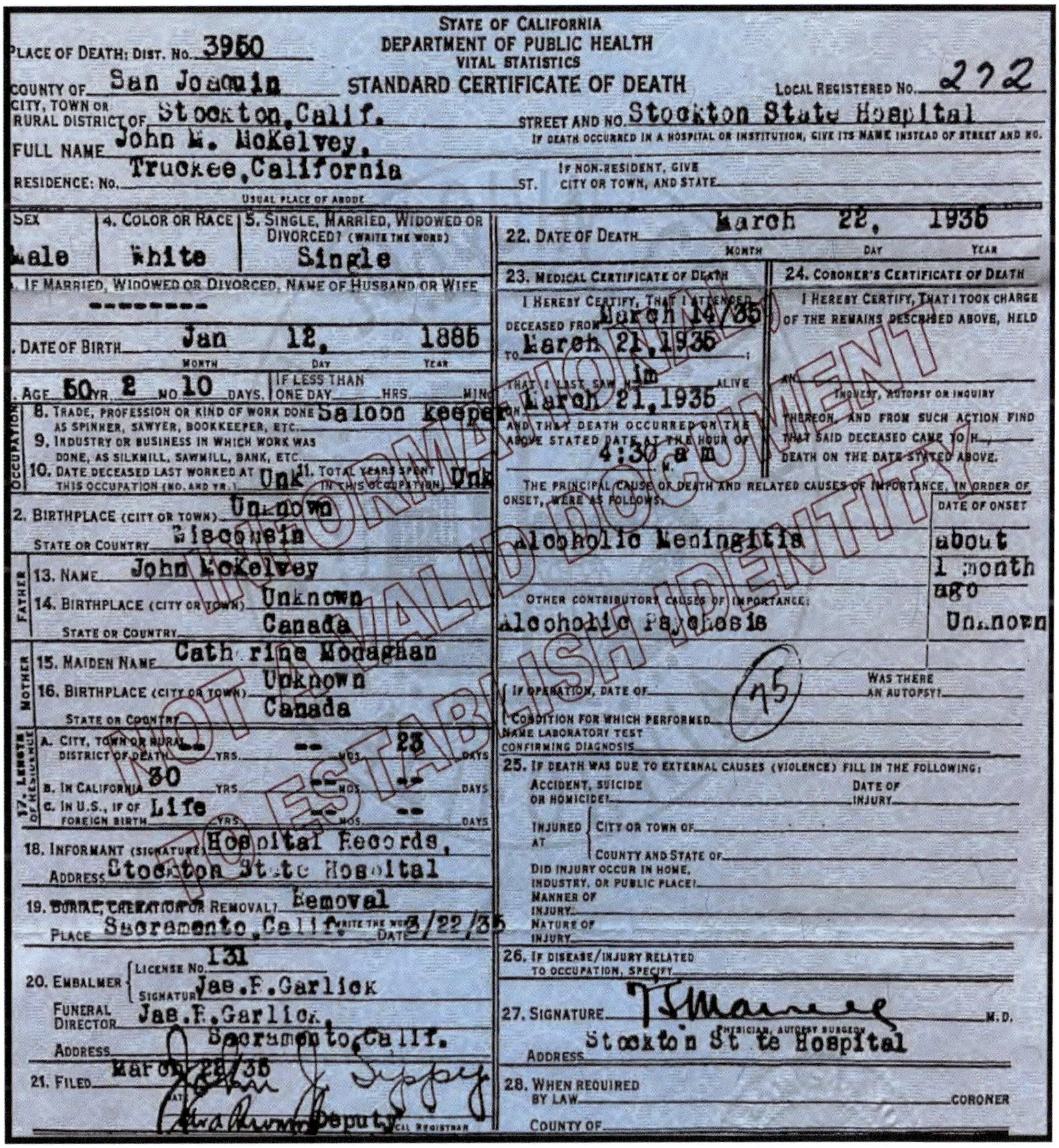

STATE OF CALIFORNIA
DEPARTMENT OF PUBLIC HEALTH
VITAL STATISTICS
STANDARD CERTIFICATE OF DEATH

PLACE OF DEATH: DIST. NO. 3950
LOCAL REGISTERED NO. 272
COUNTY OF San Joaquin
CITY, TOWN OR RURAL DISTRICT OF Stockton, Calif.
STREET AND NO. Stockton State Hospital
IF DEATH OCCURRED IN A HOSPITAL OR INSTITUTION, GIVE ITS NAME INSTEAD OF STREET AND NO.
FULL NAME John M. McKelvey.
RESIDENCE: NO. Truckee, California ST. (USUAL PLACE OF ABODE)
IF NON-RESIDENT, GIVE CITY OR TOWN, AND STATE

SEX Male
4. COLOR OR RACE White
5. SINGLE, MARRIED, WIDOWED OR DIVORCED? (WRITE THE WORD) Single
IF MARRIED, WIDOWED OR DIVORCED, NAME OF HUSBAND OR WIFE --------
DATE OF BIRTH Jan 12, 1886 (MONTH, DAY, YEAR)
AGE 50 YR. 2 MO. 10 DAYS. IF LESS THAN ONE DAY ___ HRS. ___ MIN.
OCCUPATION
8. TRADE, PROFESSION OR KIND OF WORK DONE AS SPINNER, SAWYER, BOOKKEEPER, ETC. Saloon keeper
9. INDUSTRY OR BUSINESS IN WHICH WORK WAS DONE, AS SILKMILL, SAWMILL, BANK, ETC.
10. DATE DECEASED LAST WORKED AT THIS OCCUPATION (MO. AND YR.) Unk
11. TOTAL YEARS SPENT IN THIS OCCUPATION Unk
12. BIRTHPLACE (CITY OR TOWN) Unknown
STATE OR COUNTRY Wisconsin
FATHER
13. NAME John McKelvey
14. BIRTHPLACE (CITY OR TOWN) Unknown
STATE OR COUNTRY Canada
MOTHER
15. MAIDEN NAME Cath rine Monaghan
16. BIRTHPLACE (CITY OR TOWN) Unknown
STATE OR COUNTRY Canada
17. LENGTH OF RESIDENCE
A. CITY, TOWN OR RURAL DISTRICT OF DEATH -- YRS. -- MOS. 23 DAYS
B. IN CALIFORNIA 30 YRS. -- MOS. -- DAYS
C. IN U.S., IF OF FOREIGN BIRTH Life YRS. -- MOS. -- DAYS
18. INFORMANT (SIGNATURE) Hospital Records,
ADDRESS Stockton State Hospital
19. BURIAL, CREMATION OR REMOVAL? Removal
PLACE Sacramento, Calif. DATE 3/22/36
20. EMBALMER LICENSE NO. 131
SIGNATURE Jas. F. Garlick
FUNERAL DIRECTOR Jas. F. Garlick.
ADDRESS Sacramento, Calif.
21. FILED March 23/36
John J. Sippy
Deputy ... Local Registrar

22. DATE OF DEATH March 22, 1936 (MONTH, DAY, YEAR)
23. MEDICAL CERTIFICATE OF DEATH
I HEREBY CERTIFY, THAT I ATTENDED DECEASED FROM March 14/36 TO March 21, 1936; THAT I LAST SAW him ALIVE ON March 21, 1936 AND THAT DEATH OCCURRED ON THE ABOVE STATED DATE AT THE HOUR OF 4:30 a m.
THE PRINCIPAL CAUSE OF DEATH AND RELATED CAUSES OF IMPORTANCE, IN ORDER OF ONSET, WERE AS FOLLOWS:
Alcoholic Meningitis — DATE OF ONSET: about 1 month ago
OTHER CONTRIBUTORY CAUSES OF IMPORTANCE:
Alcoholic Psychosis — Unknown
IF OPERATION, DATE OF
CONDITION FOR WHICH PERFORMED
WAS THERE AN AUTOPSY?
NAME LABORATORY TEST CONFIRMING DIAGNOSIS
75
24. CORONER'S CERTIFICATE OF DEATH
I HEREBY CERTIFY, THAT I TOOK CHARGE OF THE REMAINS DESCRIBED ABOVE, HELD AN INQUEST, AUTOPSY OR INQUIRY THEREON, AND FROM SUCH ACTION FIND THAT SAID DECEASED CAME TO H___ DEATH ON THE DATE STATED ABOVE.
25. IF DEATH WAS DUE TO EXTERNAL CAUSES (VIOLENCE) FILL IN THE FOLLOWING:
ACCIDENT, SUICIDE OR HOMICIDE? DATE OF INJURY
INJURED AT: CITY OR TOWN OF; COUNTY AND STATE OF
DID INJURY OCCUR IN HOME, INDUSTRY, OR PUBLIC PLACE?
MANNER OF INJURY
NATURE OF INJURY
26. IF DISEASE/INJURY RELATED TO OCCUPATION, SPECIFY
27. SIGNATURE T. Maness M.D. (PHYSICIAN, AUTOPSY SURGEON)
ADDRESS Stockton State Hospital
28. WHEN REQUIRED BY LAW ___ CORONER
COUNTY OF

INFORMATIONAL, NOT A VALID DOCUMENT TO ESTABLISH IDENTITY

The newspaper article on the left below includes information provided by John's sister, Mrs. W. A. Denton, a resident of Alpena, MI. The information about John is not correct. John's brother Lawrence was involved in the saloon business in Truckee and Nevada (not "the real estate business in San Francisco"), and John worked for his brother as a bartender. The newspaper article on the right correctly reports that John, a long-time resident of Truckee, CA, died in Stockton, CA. He was buried in St. Mary's Lawn Cemetery in Sacramento.

March 23, 1935, *Alpena (MI) News*

John McKelvey, Former Resident, Dies in California

The death of John McKelvey, former resident of this city, occurred suddenly Friday at his home in San Francisco, Calif., according to a message received by his sister Mrs. W. A. Denton. Death was due to pneumonia.

John McKelvey was the son of the late Mr. and Mrs. John McKelvey, pioneer residents of this city and lived here during his boyhood and youth, leaving here about 30 years ago to engage in business in the west with his brother, Lawrence McKelvey with whom he made his home. He was unmarried. The two brothers were engaged in the real estate business in San Francisco and no intimation had been given Alpena friends of Mr. McKelvey's illness which evidently was of sudden origin.

Surviving relatives are his sisters Mrs. Denton of Alpena; Mrs. Guy D. Henry of Beverly Hills, Calif.; Mrs. Charles Courtney and Mrs. George Kelly both of Deteroit and his brother, Lawrence McKelvey.

Funeral services and interment will be in San Francisco.

March 23, 1935, *Sacramento Bee*

Services Are Arranged For John M. McKelvey

Funeral services will be conducted Monday morning in the James R. Garlick Palm Chapel for John M. McKelvey, 50, a bartender in Truckee, who died yesterday in Stockton.

The interment will take place in St. Mary's Lawn Cemetery.

McKelvey, a native of Wisconsin, leaves four sisters, Mrs. G. D. Henry of Los Angeles, Mrs. George Kelley of Detroit, Mrs. Kittie Courtney of New York and Mrs. Al Denten of Michigan.

A brother, L. P. McKelvey, is connected with Cal-Neva, a resort on the boundary line of California and Nevada.

On Passing a Graveyard

by John O'Donahue (1956-2008)

May perpetual light shine upon
The faces of all who rest here.
May the lives they lived
Unfold further in spirit.
May all their past travail
Find ease in the kindness of clay.
May the remembering earth
Mind every memory they brought.
May the rains from the heavens
Fall gently upon them.
May the wildflowers and grasses
Whisper their wishes into light.
May we reverence the village of presence
In the stillness of the silent field.

From *To Bless the Space Between Us*

O'Donohue was a poet, mystic, and priest. A native Irish speaker, he was born in Western Ireland.

John M. McKelvey

BIRTH 12 Jan 1885
Eau Claire, Eau Claire County, Wisconsin, USA

DEATH 22 Mar 1935 (aged 50)
San Francisco County, California, USA

BURIAL Saint Mary's Catholic Cemetery and Mausoleum
Sacramento, Sacramento County, California, USA

Printed in Great Britain
by Amazon

53099033R00053